On the Wing

On the Wing

The Life of Birds:
From Feathers to Flight

BRUCE BROOKS

CHARLES SCRIBNER'S SONS

New York

Charles Scribner's Sons
Macmillan Publishing Company
866 Third Avenue, New York, NY 10022
Collier Macmillan Canada, Inc.

Library of Congress Cataloging-in-Publication Data
Brooks, Bruce.
    On the wing/Bruce Brooks.
        p.   cm.
    Bibliography: p.
    Includes index.
    ISBN 0-684-19119-9
    1. Birds.   I. Title.
QL673.B86   1989
598—dc19   89-4200   CIP

Macmillan books are available at special discounts for bulk purchases
for sales promotions, premiums, fund-raising, or educational use.
For details, contact:

Special Sales Director
Macmillan Publishing Company
866 Third Avenue
New York, NY 10022

10 9 8 7 6 5 4 3 2 1

Frontispiece: *Snowy egrets.*
Title Page: *Sooty tern.*

Photo credits appear on page 191.
Photo research by Robert Brow
Book design by Nancy Sugihara

Printed in the United States of America

For Anne Brooks, Gus Ben David, and Foster Silva

Contents

Acknowledgments

Thanks to: James Shreeve, who set a wonderful example for this book with its predecessor, *The Other Earthlings*, and who gave good advice at every stage of the writing; Marjorie Eno and Robert Brow, quick and accurate researchers who responded to every need and came up with many great facts and photos; Ken Dial, Roxie Laybourne, and Jim Brett, inspirational scientists and bird nuts; many bird-watching mentors, including Tom and Susan Godfrey, and Doug and Jennifer Hamilton; the people who marshaled the project that became the book—Leonard Mayhew, Don Cutler, Beatrice Rehl, David Wolff, Robert Stewart, and, especially, Erika Goldman. As with my other books, I am grateful to my wife, Penelope, my son, Alexander, and my agent, Gail Hochman, for their support and responsiveness.

Thanks also to those who make the *Nature* series possible: George Page and David Heely at WNET/New York, with the generous support of the American Gas Association, Siemens, and Public Television Stations.

Introduction

There are not many activities we can do over and over again from childhood to later life without losing the innocent wonder that drew us in the first time. We learn to zero in on the secret attractions of things and explain them, and thus we grow harder to surprise; we learn habits of perception that tempt us to focus on the familiar and ignore differences, and thus grow harder to fascinate. This happens to us with the seasons, the arts, the food we eat, the people we see. But it never seems to happen with watching animals. If a fox suddenly walks across the front yard, we stand and watch with the blank bliss of a five-year-old, and will do so every time it returns.

Many theories try to explain why we like to watch animals. Some say we see ourselves at a more primitive stage, and take fundamental delight in recognizing how far we have evolved. Others say we subconsciously respond to any living thing with a spirit of brotherhood (or, at least, of paternalism). Still others say we are simply fascinated by different lives beyond our immediate control—that we watch raccoons or armadillos much as we watch strangers on a crowded street.

They are all probably correct. But different animals evoke different responses from this mix of feelings; obviously it is easier to feel kinship with the chimpanzee than with the platypus, easier to want to provide for the fragile hummingbirds in our garden than for the puma roaming the edges of our pastures. But in general, with the exception of irredeemable pests such as the rat or the mosquito, we are eager for insights into the lives of animals—especially birds.

Outside of zoo animals, birds are the most attentively observed creatures in our world. This is partly because of opportunity: most of us see more of them in the wild than we do jaguars, newts, bats, terrapins, or even squirrels. Birds are all over the place, and we are especially aware of them because they can command our attention through two senses. They don't just display themselves in flight or hop around our feet on the sidewalk; they *sing* at us out of trees and bushes and other places too dark or high to see. This gives us a keener sense of their presence than we have with other animals.

But this hardly explains why so many millions of people all over the world buy binoculars and boots and field guides and telephoto lenses so they can traipse through marshes at dawn or up canyons at dusk just to glimpse a certain duck or vireo that is outside their usual ken. Or why millions of people hang feeders from their trees or balconies and sit by windows watching them. Or why an old man who has grown up in a city full of pigeons still gets a kick out of feeding one of them popcorn in a park, or why a child will stop doing almost anything to watch that pigeon eat.

Birds, for all their closeness to us, continue to fascinate us mostly with their *strangeness*. They are with us more than orangutans, but the average human being feels a lot closer to the orangutan he sees once a year in a zoo than to the chickadee he sees twice a day on his feeder. The chickadee seems to share virtually no features or behaviors with us. We cannot even begin to imagine what it feels like to be covered with feathers or to eat with a beak. What we feel when we watch a bird is *wonder*; as with any wild creature, we want to study how it works, figure out why it does the things it does. But to comprehend a creature for whom flight is a mundane affair, who builds nests out of grass and lichens, and whose heart beats 600 times a minute is an intriguing notion.

On the Wing aims to preserve that wonder, but also to establish an empathy with these winged marvels. These stories of bird physiology and behavior will show that birds do their strange things for reasons we can easily understand. It seems strange that the male satin bowerbird spends many days searching for bits of anything (flowers, stones, bottle caps, buttons) colored the same blue as its eyes, and then builds a cathedral of grass decorated with the blue baubles; but when we learn that the female bowerbird will not mate anywhere but in a blue-flecked cathedral of grass, and not with anyone whose eyes don't match the decor, we see the sense of the enterprise. It is peculiar to watch a jay stand by an anthill plucking up ants delicately and placing them, still alive, into various recesses among its feathers until we learn that the formic acid shed by crawling ants repels parasitic nits and mites that pester these birds. We marvel at a hummingbird flying around gardens collecting spiderwebs, until we see a hummingbird nest bound to a leaf with stout, shiny threads.

This book should not teach anyone to feel secure in a comprehensive knowledge about birds. It should teach us all to be delighted that we can never find out enough. This, I have discovered, is what ornithologists have in common —in fact, it is why most have chosen to be ornithologists. As one of them told me, "I never want to *know* everything: I just want to see it all out there tempting me to chase it. A complete understanding of birds is as hard to catch as a flying goldfinch." I hope *On the Wing* starts you off on a lifelong merry chase.

—Bruce Brooks

On the Wing

CHAPTER ONE

Making It All Possible: The Feather

Feathers are absolutely the first step in being a bird, more essential than beaks, claws, wings, or a pretty song. The snapping turtle's great beak could crack a hundred Brazil nuts before a wimpy-billed swift could open a single sunflower seed from your bird feeder. An iguana can scramble easily along a tree branch from which the weak-toed nighthawk would tumble if it tried just to squat. A bat could fly octagons around a kiwi or penguin, blindfolded. And nearly everyone can sing better than the blue jay.

But when it comes to feathers, all of these creatures bow to the birds. Each member of the 8,800 species of birds has thousands of feathers; not a single mammal, reptile, or amphibian possesses so much as one.

Thus feathers have become the prime distinguishing element of avian life forms. When paleontologists in Texas recently discovered a fossil they hoped to present as the oldest bird—many millions of years older than other proto-avian fossils, and possessing most of the features associated with evolution toward bird life—their claims kept snagging on one small lack. Their fossil contained no evidence of feathers. As one demurring scientist gently put it, "It's a wonderful fossil. But if I don't see a feather, I don't say 'bird.'"

There is one fossil over which everyone says "Bird!": *Archeopteryx lithographica*, dug out of a Bavarian quarry in 1861, later duplicated by several other finds. Archeopteryx is one of those exceptional fossils that freezes a nearly perfect transition in evolution. It's a lizard—a virtual dinosaur—*but* it's a bird. It has "hands" with jointed fingers, but they dangle on the end of full-fledged wings. It has jawbones and teeth, but it also has a shoulder girdle and pelvis unique to birds. It has scales, but it also has feathers.

This is no flimsy example of a couple of proto-feathers, here: Archeopteryx, 150 million years old, is covered from the crest of its head to the tip of its tail in a sophisticated variety of feathers exactly like those of birds today. None of the many fossils we have found of gliding lizards *older* than Archeopteryx had feathers at all; yet

Facing page: Lesser flamingo feathers.

Feathers are waterproof not because they are made of waterproof material: their structure alone creates a tight seal. (scarlet macaw)

here, in our first example of a feathered creature, we find perfect feathers that have been essentially untouched by the last 150 million years of evolution.

This emphasizes an odd mystique about the feather. Here is a very complicated item, unlike anything else in nature, which by itself distinguishes the largest class of vertebrate animals on earth (compared to the 8,800 bird species, there are only 4,000 mammal species and about 7,500 species of all other vertebrates together). This thing opened up new possibilities for coloration, temperature regulation, waterproofing, and, most importantly, flight. Yet for all of its colossal evolutionary importance, the feather seems to have popped onto the scene rather abruptly.

Where did it come from? No one can be certain; between the gliding lizards of the Triassic Period and Archeopteryx near the end of the Jurassic, we have discovered no crude protofeathers in fossils. The relationship between a feathered bird and a lizard is accepted, if not explained. But perhaps there is a clue in the description of Archeopteryx above, a clue we find just as clearly in today's birds: the simultaneous presence of both feathers and scales.

It may be that in looking for a forerunner of the feather, paleontologists will have to settle for the elongated, overlapping scales some of Archeopteryx's ancestors evolved as a means of keeping warm. Certainly the feather and scale have much in common—for example, both are tough protrusions of keratin produced by follicles in the skin. They coexist easily, produced by a single epidermis, as Archeopteryx and our birds show. Perhaps if Archeopteryx's feathers pointed toward the future, our birds' scales point back to the past and to links that were established there—links we can even see when we look at lizards now. The scales on the foot of the nuthatch scrabbling down your pine tree are a good deal like the scales of the chameleon under your porch (or those of the dinosaur buried four hundred feet farther down).

Opinions about details of evolution are always changing, and the feather has recently been the subject of such a change. Where theorists once assumed the light, stiff, aeronautic appendages evolved from scales so that lizards could fly, many now think they were brought on by the need of the earliest warm-blooded animals simply to keep warm. They may have evolved from scales, but

The feathers may not have been quite this crisp, but Archeopteryx had them.

Scales—produced by the same kind of cells that make feathers—show clearly birds' link with reptiles, according to some theories.

The Complete Camouflage

The rough-and-ready shrike.

Blending in with a bunch of leaves because your feathers are speckled may be camouflage enough for certain stay-at-home types. But, says the shrike, what good is hiding with your head down to a bird of *action*?

The shrike is indeed a bird of action—the smallest predator in a world full of huge hit men. It weighs 40 grams, compared to 800 grams for the common barred owl, with which it competes for mice and small birds in many North American forests. It hasn't the owl's silent wings, the falcon's sprinting speed, the eagle's violent beak. Its feet look like a wren's; no hawk claws to squeeze the life out of its prey with a single flex. It is just a wee songbird, among the robins (even *they* are half-again larger than it) and the warblers of the peaceful kingdom.

But one thing drives it to be different: it has a taste for the hunt. It wants to be up there with the big boys, not down on the ground scratching for worms. So how can it compete? The shrike competes because of all birds, it has the best *complete* cam-

they have more in common today with fur, another keratin product of skin cells.

Like fur, feathers—especially *down* feathers—make a wonderful insulator. They trap air and hold it next to the animal's body, which warms it. They stoutly resist wind and water and in hot weather can be flattened to the skin to squeeze out this insulating layer.

But even though feathers make such fine insulators, it seems a bit simplistic to claim they were just a kind of extended fur, primarily developed for insulation, and only coincidentally ouflage. Where other birds have ruffs to make them look bigger and meaner, or spots to make them look as if they're not there, every aspect of the shrike's appearance points out what it is, a visible songbird, plain and simple. The message of its feathers and physique is: I have no reason to hide. What you see is what you get.

And for a shrew or titmouse who believes that message, what it gets is *killed*. The shrike stomps through ground cover or flies around the meadow like any other bird looking for bugs. But what it's really looking for is a bigger tidbit, some small mammal or bird who accepts its presence and doesn't flee as it would from a bird of prey that *looks* like a bird of prey. The shrike sidles up and strikes, grabbing with its feet and breaking the neck with a bite at the base of the skull. It is a clean killer, eating what it kills, though not always at once: because it is too small to gulp its prey in one swallow, the shrike has the habit of laying food away, usually by sticking it on thorns or prongs of barbed wire all over its territory. It always comes back to its caches, though, and picks at them until they are gone. Its memory for hiding places has been studied, and found remarkable.

This clever hunter is much maligned by humans, even those who admire the violence of the falcon or owl. These people complain of the shrike's ignoble stealth; if you're going to kill things, they say, you should be up front about it. You should look like a meanie instead of pretending you're a good ol' songbird. They ignore the shrike's disadvantages of size and equipment; and they see nothing ignoble in the stealth of a bird pretending it's a stone or a branch to *escape* a hunter. The habit of impaling the kill has also drawn fire from the shrike's critics, as if sticking a dead mouse on a thorn were cruel and hurt the poor rodent more than tearing it to bits right away, as do other predatory birds.

The shrike, of course, is oblivious to its critics. It has a hard hunt and enjoys every edge it can gain. And it's good, too—there are 74 species of shrike surviving across the world. Yet, notwithstanding the claims that it has taken unfair advantage of the innocents of nature, the shrike doesn't seem to be burgeoning. It is not nearly as common as the finches and sparrows it occasionally kills. We have only two species in the United States—the loggerhead and the northern—and they are not all that frequently spotted by bird watchers. But perhaps we, like the ill-fated prey, are simply mistaking this knave of camouflage for yet another mockingbird or jay.

It's a good thing we aren't shrews.

useful for flight. If Archeopteryx needed only to keep warm, why didn't he grow hair and the layer of fat that usually supplements a fur coat? Hair and fat served the early cats well enough. Why wasn't it good enough for Archeopteryx?

Because Archeopteryx had a different idea

about survival and progress. The rugged do-or-die of natural selection seems to have favored those of his ancestors who moved up into trees from the ground, and then into the air between trees. These experimenters found new food, escaped the ground-dwelling heavies, and passed on to their descendants the drive toward lightness and freedom from the boundaries of habitat. Nature rewarded their experimentation and survival—with the feather.

If you want to glide between trees catching bugs, feathers are obviously superior to fat and fur. They expand the surface area you can offer to the air for support (Archeopteryx's predecessors had probably already eked from nature some elongated scales on the forelimbs and tail); they also reduce the weight you must throw in the face of that delicate support (a square foot of saber-toothed tiger integument probably weighs a couple of pounds, while a square foot of bird skin and feathers comes in at a few ounces). For all of their lightness, they are much tougher than flesh, too, in terms of surface resistance and tensile strength.

For true flight, an animal needs more than feathers. Archeopteryx lacked most of the other necessities, such as extraordinary pectoral muscles (to flap its wings) and an enlarged breastbone on which to fasten them. The bones weren't hollow for reduced weight; its heavy lizard's tail, with its twenty-one vertebrae, was no key to the skies either. For successful living on the wing, an animal needs to develop special behaviors and physical capabilities demanded by everything from prey to topography—great quickness (airborne insects have always been fleet), fantastic vision (flying brings you up fast on obstacles), a sophisticated autonomic nervous system that can adjust the performance of 20,000 feathers to a sudden zephyr. Compared to modern birds, Archeopteryx was probably pretty slow, myopic, and insensitive. If it dropped by a bird sanctuary today, it'd be outmaneuvered by everyone from the chickadee to the turkey vulture.

But for all that it lacked, Archeopteryx had one thing—one gift for its descendants, of such value that they would spread farther across the world than any other class of animal, developing the widest diet and the widest range of habitat—both of which meant thriving survival. If success in an ancestor means supporting a big family through the ages, Archeopteryx was a champion. Its one gift—the feather—has been enough for 8,800 species, and all they've had to do is pass it on, virtually without modification, just as they received it, long ago.

What Is a Feather? How Is It Made?

More than at any other time, we feel the strangeness of birds when we stop and pick up a feather in our path. There is nothing on Earth to compare it to; there is no material like it, no form, nothing that functions quite the same way.

Feathers grow straight out of follicles in the skin much the way human hair and animal fur grows. Like our hair, feathers grow only in certain places—the follicles are grouped in a pattern of tracts along the bird's body. Birds look as if they are covered everywhere only because the feathers overlap, covering the bald areas between tracts.

The first stage of a feather's incipience is a small pimple called a papilla—a kind of mound surrounded by a tiny trough. Papillae begin to appear on the skin of the embryo chick after about a week of incubation in the egg. The papilla's mound stretches into a cone, and the trough deepens around it, creating a feather follicle. By the time the chick hatches, things are happening inside the papilla. Layers form: a thin, horny sheath on the outside, then a layer of fast-growing epidermal cells (called the Malpighian) that will become the actual feather, and, innermost, a pulp of dermal cells that will supply the epidermal structure with blood as it develops.

The fast cells shift into a high gear of differentiation, and the feather as we would recognize it begins with a long series of parallel protrusions—like a wall of popsicle sticks. These sticks will be the barbs, the thin lines that project sideways from the central spike of the feather. This spike, called the rachis, will develop at the base of the barbs, from the same cells that sprouted them. Oddly, the cells get around to the rachis only after a barb has been sprung, as it were, in thin air—almost as if someone built a flagpole first, and then decided to construct a foundation at its base. At this point the new feather will become one of six types: contour, down, semi-plume, filoplume, bristle, and powder down.

The longer, stiffer feathers that cover most of the mature bird's body are the contour feathers, so-called because they define the outline of the bird. These are what most of us imagine when we use the word "feather"; down and semi-plumes are pieces of fluff that lie under the contours for insulation and padding; filoplumes are nearly hairs that appear sparsely; bristles *are* hairs, even more sparse; and powder down is a fragile substance that turns to oily dust if it is touched, even by the bird. Contour feathers hold their shape and color, even on the path or sidewalk where we find them.

Contour feathers have a straight central shaft and regular barbs that interlock neatly through a system of barbules, tiny hooks that poke from the shaft of a barb, much in the manner the barb pokes from the rachis. These tiny barbules pop out when the growing barbs push against the Malpighian sheath, as if from an irrepressible pressure for the feather to keep producing *something*. This pressure is probably a command from the thyroid gland, in the form of a secretion. The command is apparently not issued for the other types of feathers, which are fluffier or stringier and less regimental because they are free from the impeccable orderliness of barbules.

In a mature contour feather, the system of barbules is one of nature's most amazing bits of engineering. Without this purely structural device, the feather would not be waterproof or cut the air as precisely as it does in flight, nor would it interact fittingly with the feathers around it. The bird would generally be a far less flexible and creative animal. A large part of a bird's day is spent maintaining the system of barbules—for many birds, more time than is spent hunting or eating.

In an average contour feather—say a flight feather of a pigeon—there are about *600 pairs of barbs* slanting from the main shaft. Each barb

Vane, barb, and several thousand barbules, neatly hooked.

has about *500 barbules on each side*. The barbules on the upper edge of each barb possess hooks along their length; the barbules on the lower edge are straighter, ideally constructed and placed to be hooked by the barbules beneath. Thus, the top edge of one barb and the bottom edge of another are joined by a kind of zipper—thousands of hooks and rods interlocking. There are about 2,400 of these zippers in a contour feather.

Is it any wonder such a feather holds its shape? The dense, microscopic interlocking of barbules means a feather can present itself to air and water almost as a solid plane. Yet, because the plane is really an intricate construction of tiny parts—more than a million parts in each feather—it weighs only a small fraction of what a solid mass the same size would weigh. And it is far more flexible, both in construction and function. A feather can bend, rotate, whiffle in a harsh wind, and even spring back after solid impact, far better than a membrane or carapace would do. Each *barb* can bend and rotate; the whole construction is built of flexibility upon flexibility, a good part of which comes from the fact that the barbules are not hooked permanently—the zipper effect releases before the barbs would break from a severe twist or impact. If we toy with that feather we picked up, we can see this. Give it a ripple by running a finger from the tip down toward the quill. Several of the barbs separate. The feather no longer looks so taut and elegant; now it looks a bit ragged and not especially brilliant as a flying surface.

To the bird, it's nearly as bad as it looks. Feathers with gaps and curls among the barbs don't perform well—they insulate and fly with less wholeness. Apparently, they *feel* funny, too. Birds have no trouble locating which among their vast array of feathers—about 25,000 in some birds—have been ruffled.

Unless barbs have actually been torn—and they're tough—they can be realigned with a quick nibble, a combing from the foot, or a zip through the beak. Again, we can see this with any feather: running it between two fingers, from the quill up toward the tip, will restore the taut elegance we disrupted moments ago. The barbules whose hold we broke are now rehooked. The bird's maintenance of its feathers this way is called preening. Applied to humans, this word implies a vain fastidiousness, the image of someone looking in the mirror constantly, fussing with every errant curl or eyelash. In birds, however,

preening is far from an act of vanity. It is a constant, essential pursuit—the one which makes all others possible. If being a bird means having and using feathers, then being a strong survivor means taking care of them.

Preening not only realigns barbules unhooked by some accident; the feather's structural integrity may also be disrupted by dirt, fluids, and parasites. The fastening of barbules is a delicate cling between such tiny surfaces that a few specks of microscopic dust can skew the connection. A spot of sap or oil can do the same. To remove impurities, the bird grasps the feather near its base with its beak, then either nibbles along the length or pulls it through its mandibles in one motion. Usually the bird fluffs its body feathers outward so that it can reach the individual units cleanly, because feathers are preened one at a time.

Preening is so important that most birds have been equipped with a special chemical dispensary to aid in the process: the uropygial (or preen) gland. This double-lobed gland near the base of the tail is the largest of the very few skin glands a bird possesses; in some birds it appears to be the only skin gland. It has a nipple-like orifice, and upon pressure from the beak it yields an oily substance the bird spreads through the feathers (and in some cases, on the feet) with its beak.

The composition of the oil varies from bird to bird, as does the extent of the oil's effects. The large running birds—emu, ostrich, cassowary, bustard—and some woodpeckers and pigeons have no preen gland at all. In the nightjars, the gland is barely functional. Yet the fatty, waxy secretion of some waterfowl seems important in keeping these birds fully warm and waterproof, even though the feathers are structurally waterproof without the coating. Other waterfowl— the anhinga and cormorant, which swim with their bodies completely beneath the surface of water—have a dinky gland, and get soaked; they must hang themselves out to dry after a swim, standing on rocks or branches with the wings spread open. Because they swim fully immersed, they wouldn't *want* to be buoyant.

Wing feathers, constantly buffeted, need constant preening, whether for flying or (in the case of this chinstrap penguin) swimming.

Dead on the Head

Sometimes we have used feathers almost as birds do—Eskimos made robes of them for warmth; other American Indians displayed them in ceremonies of aggression or sexual competition; hunters placed them on arrow shafts to improve aerodynamics; campers stuffed them in sleeping bags and coats for insulation.

But throughout history our biggest plundering of feathers has been for the sheer decoration of one item of apparel that itself was nothing but a bagatelle: the lady's hat.

It is difficult today to believe that in the late-nineteenth and early-twentieth centuries, the relatively minor millinery industry in Europe and North America could wipe out species after species of birds, many of whom sported only a few desirable plumes, just for the sake of high fashion. Those hats with the dopey dyed feathers—they just look too *silly* to cause much harm.

But they did. There were a lot of heads to be hatted, and when fashion dicatated they should be adorned with an arching plume or a splash of iridescent feathers— or even with an entire albatross wing or barn-owl head—hunters went off into the country or down to the shore to supply the market. The numbers, when they were kept, are astonishing. In England alone, between December 1884 and April 1885 the remains of 404,464 West Indian and Brazilian birds and 356,389 East Indian birds were sold. In the first three years of World War I, when a bill to prohibit import was in a Parliament committee, nearly 2 million pounds of feathers (excluding ostrich) were imported, valued at more than a pound sterling per pound of weight.

One year the ladies were wearing fairy terns, sprayed green and fetchingly mounted.

Most of the extravagant plumes were borne by birds during the nesting season, which was terrific for the hunters: it is a time when birds keep pretty still, often hanging around one place, and are easy prey.

The feather harvest during nesting had disastrous consequences. Removal of a parent at nesting time wipes out a whole family; when the hunters descend for a few years in a row, whole colonies can be wiped out. The hunters, oblivious to the depletion of their resource, moved from colony to colony and soon eliminated entire species. No matter: as soon as the egret feather dried up on the market, designers moved on to the bird of paradise or the great albatross. Fashion can adjust to nature much better than nature adjusts to fashion.

The plumes of the snowy egret almost doomed the species.

Alfred Newton, a founder of the British Ornithological Union and a zoology professor at Cambridge, first drew critical attention to the plunder of native birds in 1868. The next year, Parliament passed laws closing hunting season for three months for 33 seabirds. In the United States, several individual states passed laws in the 1870s to regulate slaughter, but until they were united against interstate commerce under federal acts much later, these were relatively ineffective. In 1886, George Bird Grinnell (yes, George Bird Grinnell) founded the Audubon Society to initiate protection of non-game birds and wildlife, especially over the plumage issue. "Very slowly," he said, "the public are awakening to see that the fashion of wearing the feathers and skins of birds is abominable."

(continued)

Very slowly indeed. Well into the next century, even after laws and international trade treaties banned feather traffic between agreeing nations, the public showed little sign of slackening its demand for exotic feathers to jazz up its toppers. The effect of laws in the United States and Europe was simply to drive hunters to the tropics, where they found fabulous birds in full nuptial plumage, most of them on uninhabited islands where they had not developed wariness of humans. Many species were brought to the edge of extinction for their feathers, though not as many as were wiped out by the destruction of their habitat.

In the 1970s many nations finally took stock of what they were losing, and began to pass prohibitive regulations. In 1975 an important agreement was ratified by member nations at the Convention on International Trade in Endangered Species (CITES): commercial trade in rare or endangered birds was prohibited or heavily restricted. Separate U.S. tariffs and bans nixed the import of certain birds and their "products."

Today in the United States it is illegal to possess or wear any wild bird feathers, with a limited exception for "the making of fishing flies and similar commercial uses." Use of the feathers of domestic birds (chickens, ducks, pheasants) is okay, as is the collection of down from several wild birds. The use of eiderdown is regulated; eiders almost disappeared when down thieves took from the ducks' nests the soft feathers necessary for the incubation and hatching of the eggs. At least one bird that once suffered terrible hunting in the wild—the ostrich—has been domesticated and bred for its plumes, which are plucked from the flightless wings twice a year. And used, quite often, for hats.

The effects of the preen gland's oil go beyond the immediate gloss it imparts to the bird's feathers and beak. In many birds the secretion contains a chemical that turns into vitamin D when it is activated by sunlight. The vitamin in the feathers is absorbed by the skin, or swallowed as the bird nibbles its feathers. Researchers removing preen glands from experimental groups of birds have shown that some species tend to develop rickets without their dose of vitamin D. This, and the fact that a nibble is not always enough to get rid of the substances mucking up the feathers, is one reason birds take sunbaths. Emerging into bright sunlight from shade, a bird may suddenly flop onto the ground with a gasp, like a landlocked tourist arriving at the beach after a long drive. This ecstatic pose often seems to be involuntary—sunshine hits and the bird sprawls. It fluffs its feathers and spreads them to the sun, sometimes turning its head to fix the sun with a stare. The sun warms the skin, softens oils in the feathers, and drives parasites to dark spots under the wings, whence they can be removed easily during the preening that follows the sunbath.

Birds also bathe in water and dust. Most land birds will use any small patch of water to bathe in—shallows alongside a river or pond, pools of melted snow, even the beads of water on a large leaf after a rainstorm. Some birds bathe standing up, by leaning into the water, dipping their heads and tails, thrashing their wings, and generally ruffling around. Others, such as the goshawk, walk into a few inches of water, lift their tails rather inelegantly, and sit down with a plop. Swifts and swallows, the most aerial of birds, take their baths without ceasing to fly—they dip or skim and preen without missing a wing beat.

If there's no water standing about, many birds will take a shower in the rain. The most extravagant of these is the parrot, which will hang upside down to get fully wet. Once the bath or shower is over, the bird flies to a perch and preens. The water has loosened some of the dirt in the feathers and on the skin, allowing the preening to proceed more effectively.

However, sometimes smudges of dirt and oil—and especially lice and fleas—cannot be dislodged by sun or water. To get at these, the bird will find a patch of dry dirt or sand, scoop out a shallow groove, and settle into it, breast down. Flapping wings raise clouds of gritty dust, which the bird welcomes with fluffed feathers. It may then roll in the dirt like a dog, getting good and filthy; or it may neatly toss dirt onto its back with its beak. Once the feathers have a rough coating of dust, the bird stands up, fluffs the feathers and gives them a good shake. Whatever dust remains on the feathers, the bird then preens away. The dust has probably absorbed excess oils on the skin or feathers. It has also driven out some of the ectoparasites—lice, fleas, larvae, and ticks—which found the dust-free bird a commodious host, but packed up and left when the grit began to fly.

All of these baths are preludes to the preening—this constant routine of beaksmanship is what keeps the feathers fit. However, there are some obvious places a bird cannot reach with its beak. And though it can scratch head and neck

Even seabirds bathe up a splash. (red-tailed tropic bird)

A bobwhite quail prefers dust to water.

with its feet—herons, with long expanses of neck out of bounds to their long beaks, even have a preening comb on one toe—such digital preening doesn't do the job a beak does. So many birds turn to their mates for help, leaning their faces toward each other for mutual preening of the face and neck. In some owls, this is especially important—the flat facial disks of these birds, made up of small, sensitive feathers, gather sound in the dark and improve their nocturnal hunting Dirt, fleas, and ragged barbs would certainly interfere with acoustic sensitivity.

It is not surprising that the feather, with its delicate tentacles extended into the still air, should be able to register a ripple of sound waves and pass it on to the bird's ear. (After all, some of the more sensitive antennae of moths look like crude feathers.) It's simply another remarkable feat of these masterpieces of strength and refinement.

Out with the Old, in with the New

A mature feather is not living; as soon as it reaches its full development, the blood supply that ran through the shaft is cut off, and the feather stiffens in the follicle at its base. The follicle is surrounded by muscles in the skin, and through these the feather's movement is controlled—its adjustments to hold air for heat or flatten for cooling, its responses to the movements of wind in flight, its ruffling for mating displays. Feathers are controlled with remarkable subtlety and precision, owing to the thorough system of muscles. A Canada goose has more than 12,000 skin muscles just for feather control.

Muscles move the follicle, which in turn moves the feather in its sheath. Eventually, when there is no lively adhesion from the feather's quill, no expansion within the fatigued grasp of the follicle, the feather begins to loosen. Also, during

An anhinga milks its preen gland.

The face of an owl is a disk for receiving sound, with each feather a receptor cell.
(short-eared owl)

the feather's term of service, its tips have been getting pretty battered, especially those of the wing and tail—the most important feathers for flight. Takeoffs and landings on rough bark, flights through trees and bushes, hops through sharp-edged grasses, harsh twists from blustery winds—all of these things contribute to a wearing away of the barbs on the ends of the contour feathers.

Fortunately, replacements are always at the ready. Behind every mature feather—slightly nudged into a hole in the end of the quill and deep in the follicle—is the bud of a new feather waiting for its chance to sprout. Once the worn feather begins to loosen, it may fall out spontaneously, the bird may pluck it out, or it may simply yield to the pressure from the bud that is next in line. In every case, the old feather goes and the new feather grows.

Feathers that are lost at odd times during the year are replaced in this way. But a bird does not wait for the wear and tear to take its toll haphazardly. Instead, at least once a year, a bird loses its old feathers in a regular sequence of shedding called a molt. Most birds molt often during their first year. On the way from their natal down in early summer to their *first nuptial* (or breeding) plumage the following spring, they pass through a *juvenal* phase in which their wing and tail feathers are mature enough for flight but their bodily feathers retain a downy fluff, and a *first winter* plumage, when all of their feathers are mature but undistinguished by the special coloration of the breeding phase. This first winter plumage comes in time for the bird's first migration.

For mature birds, the number of molts per year differs among species; some change plumage three times a year, some only once. Within a species, molts differ according to several variables—season and weather, gender, state of health, and location of habitat. The sequence and duration of a molt also differs for every species. The golden eagle takes its time shedding feathers, especially the flight feathers (called remiges);

The whippoorwill is ready for a molt: note the gouges worn from the primary flight feathers and tail.

it retains some of them for two or three years, while others are replaced and brought into full play so that the bird will never be weakened in its aggressive flight. The flightless penguins tend to lose all of their feathers in a kind of fire sale, lasting as little as two weeks. These cold-weather birds only begin their molt when the new plumage is well on the way, so they will never be

Feather Racket

The physics of feathers and air bring up a variation on the old conundrum about a tree falling in a forest: If a feather flaps at 2,000 feet over the Indian Ocean and nobody hears it, did it make a sound?

Well, of course feathers *do* make sounds when they cut the air, and of course birds *hear* them. So do the animals birds prey upon, if they are alert: a wary mouse risking a trip across a marsh keeps its ears open for the flutter of the kestrel, and can probably distinguish it from the flutter of the kingfisher. But among birds, the small wisps of noise that come from regular flight do not carry any special sonic meaning—they make up a kind of white noise in the bird world. A few crafty birds have gone further with the possibilities of sound, expanding their behavior into the realm of feather acoustics. They have discovered ways of making distinctive sounds by manipulating certain feathers in a certain way. With some birds, this occurs during flight, when a steady rush of air is easy to come by; others work harder, creating their whirls of air on the ground.

Almost all of the feather music is made by males for purposes of "display"—to warn other males away and impress females during courtship. Hummingbirds—whose 70 wing beats per second give them their name and probably make them our noisiest decibel-per-ounce bird in normal flight—create screeches with their wings and tails during courtship dives. So do snipes. Nighthawks take spectacular plummets from 100 feet in the air, waiting until the last moment to pull out of the dive; they emphasize the melodrama with a loud, burred wail of wind through the wings, right out of a grade-B spook movie. Woodcocks have evolved three narrowed primary flight feathers that whistle and twitter, most dramatically during display flights, but also when the bird is flushed and frightened. Several grouse and snipes stand on the ground or on a log and perform the misnamed music of "drumming" which, despite its percussive sound, is not produced by any kind of solid striking—the birds simply whip their wing feathers rapidly and intricately through the air.

The short-eared owl courts with a flight featuring a little applause: at the end of his swooping dive he stretches his wings behind his back and claps them a few times.

without the remarkable insulation that lets them maintain a 110° body temperature in a −75° environment. Once the molt starts, the penguin may even stand in one place for the duration, shucking feathers in a circle around its erect body.

Most birds molt more privately, retreating into a protected spot after the breeding season, losing their feathers over the course of several weeks and waiting for new feathers to mature. The quest for privacy is not prompted by modesty. A molting bird is a weakened bird. Flight is hampered, and a ragged appearance shows this clearly to predators. Also, most birds eat much less during molting, losing stamina and body weight in the draining process of replacing the feathers that usually make up about a quarter of their mass. For example, many penguins fast completely

Silent flight means owls can sneak up on things. (great gray owl)

Whether he is lauding his mate-to-be or his own wingsmanship is unknown. Some nightjars will do this same clapping trick while circling the head of a human who has come too close to a nest.

This noisiness is most unlike an owl, however. Far from evolving equipment and techniques to create new sounds, owls have come up with special tools for silence. Most of them hunt at night, in the dark quiet of woods and fields, and the noise of their flapping flight would alarm their prey if it weren't for the serration of the feathers on the leading edge of their huge wings. The sawtooth pattern breaks up the rush of air over the surface just enough to silence it. Also, the trailing surface of the owl's primaries has a looser, softer edge than on other birds, letting the air ease off the wings instead of snapping abruptly. The sound eliminated in this way is of course very tiny per feather. But these increments of "noise saved," feather by feather and wing beat by wing beat, allow the stealthy owl to hunt in silence.

during their molts. Such abstemiousness reflects more than a limited capability to find food; growing feathers seems simply to take a lot of energy.

There is an obvious area of feather-function that goes quite beyond the merely mechanical, however; a feather may require replacement even though it is intact as an insulator or flight tool. This is because feathers don't just *do*; they *show*. Birds have a more fabulous array of colors than any other class of vertebrate, and the colors come entirely from their feathers. Color is important to all birds, not just the electric parrots and peacocks. Rare is the bird whose dull yellow bill is its brightest characteristic—even the plain brownish songbirds we see everywhere present to the careful viewer a sophisticated pattern of light and dark bars and speckles, cool and hot flashes of russet and gold, subtle illusions of shad-

Flight during a molt can be a ragged ride. (triton cockatoo)

ing, brash spots of contrast. Almost any contour feather we pick up demonstrates this variety of coloration. Few feathers are truly monochrome.

Like everything else about feathers, color is not as simple as it looks. We would expect those Dufy blues, Matisse reds, and Van Gogh yellows to be made of pigments. But there are few colors that come just from pigmentation. Most are produced or heightened by structural features. Barbs and barbules are individually coated with precise horny thicknesses (perhaps thinnesses would be a better word) designed to reflect and refract light to create color effects. Just as a glass prism breaks up invisible sunlight and shows a rainbow, a microscopic patina on a line of white barbs can show a pure, radiant violet or green or black-and-yellow variegation. Some color effects come from the wearing away of feather tips,

as in the snow bunting: the tips are unpigmented, presenting an unbroken whiteness when they are new; but in the course of a winter the tips wear away, leaving the deeper-hued bases to show through, darkening the bird's overall appearance. The reverse is true, though much less dramatic, in several species.

Because pigmented barbs are tougher than unpigmented, some light-colored herons, pelicans, storks, and gulls have evolved thin bands of pigment on their wing tips, the feather areas most vulnerable to wear. When these tips wear away, the birds brighten. Most colors are conveyed by a combination of pigment, coating, and structural position. For example, iridescence (in hummingbirds, peacocks, and pigeons) is produced by a pigment overlaid with diffractive coatings that brighten it, further heightened into

The painted bunting seems to come from the palette of a Fauvist.

the illusion of luminosity by flattened barbules twisted 90° horizontally to better reflect light. This incredibly complex micro-architecture is what makes the color seem to hover above the feather. An opposite angling—with a vertical bias— produces the velvety appearance of some feathers, as the vertical barbules absorb light to look deep and soft.

Precision and subtlety of design are most striking in close observation. A single barbule often contains several colors produced in different ways. A layer of yellow keratin on a barbule made blue by structure produces a parrot's green; those iridescent barbules on the peacock are covered with *three* layers of keratin, each less than half a micron thick. The namesake color of the blue jay comes not from a pigment, but from tiny solid particles, suspended in transparent cells on the upper side of the barbules, which shatter sunlight and absorb all wavelengths but blue. Within the complexity of this production of blue, of course, the feathers also produce the required stripes of black and tips of white.

The well-defined iridescence of a peacock feather.

Good Bugs and Bad Bugs

Preening, bathing, and plain old scratching help to curtail many of the parasites that infest a bird's feathers and flesh. The larger pests—lice, fleas, ticks—are easiest to locate and remove. The bugs need to sustain themselves by trips from the feathers to the bird's skin, and their bites draw attention to their location.

One pest, however, seems to feed directly on feather tissue itself. Mites, smaller than the bloodthirsty insects, hide themselves among the barbules and munch the nerveless surfaces of feathers. Mites are harder for the bird to find—they do not betray themselves with painful bites into the flesh as they move around the relatively large area of feathers. Also, the baths birds take to discourage insect pests seem to have less effect on mites.

But the bird kingdom has a natural mite-icide. Somewhere along the line of evolution a brainy jay or thrush or wild turkey discovered that formic acid killed mites. Formic acid is produced and secreted by ants, which, when crawling among the feathers, leave behind this chemical as they are rubbed and scratched by the barbules.

Today "anting" is a worldwide practice for more than 200 species. There are several techniques: some birds pick up ants with their bill and crush them, then pass the ant over the feathers with a thoroughness reminiscent of preening; some birds do the same with a live ant held in the bill; many birds pluck ants and place them in among the feathers, where they crawl around; others flop on anthills with wings outspread, to let the ants crawl where they will—the ants in the feathers are eventually removed with the bill. Oddly enough, most insectivorous birds discard the ants they have used.

Birds finding themselves short of ants will use, instead, a fantastic variety of objects and substances, most of them acidic in some way. Some of the substitutes are: land snails, beetles, termites, bees, mothballs, cigarette butts, chokecherries, and walnut meats. One tame magpie regularly took an ant in its bill, flew to its owner's shoulder while he was smoking his pipe, dipped the ant in the pipe bowl, and proceeded to rub it on its feathers.

The variety of substances and practices leads some ornithologists to look beyond the purely pesticidal aspect of "anting." They speculate that the practice may have something to do with skin irritation during molting, though they are unable to say how a mothball or an ant covered with hot Balkan Sobranie ash soothes the epidermis.

In a few cases, colors are directly related to diet. There was a time when flamingos in captivity kept turning white, to the consternation of a lot of zoo keepers. Everybody knows flamingos are supposed to be pink. But birds that had a brilliant blush when they arrived shed their color soon thereafter, though they stayed perfectly healthy. In many zoos the birds were not enclosed, so the bleaching had nothing to do with a lack of sunlight. What was it? After trying many things, someone had the idea of restoring to the zoo birds' diet certain crustaceans they fed on in the wild, and *voilà*—the feathers bloomed like roses. The "pinkening" agents in the crus-

The wood duck is a spectacular assembly of effects.

taceans were later isolated—carotenoids—and they are now included in special "flamingo food" on the animal chow market.

A certain crimson pigment (turacin) in the wings of South American plantain-eating touracos confounded a biologist who caught a bird by the wing in a rainstorm, and was left, after the bird slipped through his grasp, with bloody hands. At least they *looked* bloody; the scientist found that the stain was in fact the wing pigment, which washed from his skin as easily as it had from the bird. He caught three more birds in the next rainstorm, and laundered them all to a pale pink. Later analysis of the gelatinous pigment revealed that it held a high level of pure copper. Thus touracos gained two distinctions: they are the only birds who get their color from

copper and the only ones whose color is water-soluble.

Why do birds take such pains to produce their sophisticated arrangements of colors? Certainly not just to please us with their prettiness; our eyes are the least of their concerns. Other eyes, however, are everything to birds: those of their predators, their prey, and their own species. Birds have enemies. Alligators gobble up egrets with a crash of the jaws; snapping turtles snatch ducklings on the water from below. The common marmoset will grab a small bird from a tree limb. The kit fox will sneak up on a ground nest at night. Pythons drop from vines onto feeding birds and swallow them whole. Almost any carnivore will eat a nestling bird, and every animal from a squirrel to a lizard will snack on eggs.

Of course, birds have plenty of predators within their own kingdom. There is such a wide range of sizes among birds, and such a large number of birds of prey, that birds practically make a food chain by themselves. The chickadee falls to the shrike, which in turn may be eaten by the Cooper's hawk. A great horned owl kills the Cooper's hawk and eats it before a golden eagle lunches on the huge owl. The last laugh belongs to a turkey vulture who finds the eagle's carcass and metabolizes the residues of all his previous unfortunate feathered mates.

The art of not being seen is the first line of defense for many birds. But birds can't just lie back in a hollow tree—they must eat a tremendous amount to keep their high metabolisms buzzing, and thus spend most of their time out in the open looking for food. Feathers are obviously the key to being overlooked in activity.

The elegant camouflage that birds have developed is a marvel of evolution. The most common tricky plumage is that which allows the motionless bird to blend in with the prevalent background in its habitat. In most cases, the success of the camouflage depends on a complementary behavior. The gray, choppy-textured frogmouths stick their beaks in the air, close their eyes, and lean their stiffened bodies to imitate the angled branches of the trees they live in: having plumage like bark is no good unless you behave like a bough. Nightjars hunker down among the leaves of the forest floor and are often nearly trod upon by surprised bird watchers who thought they were keeping a sharp eye out. Bitterns, with breasts striped in imitation of the reeds they live in, stick their beaks straight up like just another stem of marsh grass and hold this posture unrelentingly. One naturalist in England found a bittern in this posture and circled it, only to find the bittern pivoting exactly with him, to keep its striped side always in non-sight.

Some feathers do more than blend a bird in

There are two tawny frogmouths in this picture.

The art of not being seen: black skimmer chicks disappear in their "nest"; the ostrich can lower its neck and become a boulder; the snowy owl can hunt boldly in daylight; noddy terns imitate the disruptive patterns of rocky shores.

with its surroundings—they create optical illusions. Many ground-feeding birds have developed a light-belly/dark-back pattern, which has the effect of de-emphasizing shadows that show the roundness of their bodies. This effect, called countershading, seems to subtract the dimension of depth and leaves the birds flat against the mottled background. The countershaded bird is nearly invisible.

More accurately, it's invisible as long as it stays *still*. Most postures of disappearance depend on the freeze; invisibility in motion is a bit much to ask for. Some birds, however, sport patterns that gain them a second of *reduced* visibility when they are moving—and a second is often plenty of time to save a bird's life. One of the small black-and-white woodpeckers—say, the hairy, or the downy—will be a speckled blur as

Damage

The most natural feather damage comes from simple wear or impact that tears or breaks the feather. But there are other "natural causes."

A young bird who suffers even a brief spell of malnutrition—which can be common during the days of high-protein need—will suffer from *fault bars* in its plumage (also called *hunger traces*). They are like weak links in the chain of cells making up the growing feather. Because feathers grow from the base rather than from the tip—that is, the tip is the oldest part of the feather, with newer growth accruing behind it—the faults show clearly as points of retarded growth in exactly the same spot on all feathers. The feather will break easily along the lines of a fault; once one feather breaks, pressure increases on the feather next to it, which breaks at the same point, and so on. The truncated feathers will be replaced at the next molt, but in the meantime they can severely inhibit a bird's flight.

Falconers take matters into their own hands and repair fault bars by a process called *imping*. A feather from a previous molt is cut to mimic the outer part of the faulted feather. The faulted feather is then snapped off at the weak point and the surrogate part is fitted to the part that is still in the bird; the two parts are attached by a doubled-ended blade, an imping needle, one end of which is pushed into the shaft of the new feather while the other end is pushed into the shaft of the broken one on the bird. Imped feathers hold pretty well. In any case, they are better than half-feathers, and see the bird through to the next molt.

Probably the worst *unnatural* scourge of feathers is the floating oil that covers the water when a tanker leaks or jettisons some extra weight into the ocean, or when an industrial plant dumps its used machine oil in a river. A bad oil spill will cover hundreds of square miles of water with a layer of sludge several inches thick. Ducks and geese flying by will not distinguish the oil-covered surface from the clean water. They land, sink through the oil, and emerge—if they are lucky—completely covered with greasy petroleum.

Oil immediately destroys the integrity of the feather. The million parts no longer interlock—their surfaces slide off one another and leave the feather a stringy, flat thing void of its waterproofing and insulation functions. Of course the oiled birds cannot

it dashes through light and shadow in a forest, and this may dull the focus of a pursuing hawk just enough to throw off the timing of its otherwise fatal strike.

Nature is fair, however: some hawks gain that second back, by the same method. The barred underwings of accipiters, for example, may extend their stealth for an instant longer as they zip in on a victim whose glance upward cannot

focus clearly on the threat—until it's too late. The speedy football player Gale Sayers once told the men who blocked for him exactly what he needed to score touchdowns: "Give me eighteen inches of daylight for a second and a half and I'm gone." A goshawk might say the same: "Give me two-tenths of a second *in* daylight, and that grouse is gone."

If concealment fails to avert an attack, some-

A scaup, after a dive through an oil slick.

fly either—gaping feathers don't hold air. What an oiled bird can do, for the first time in its life, is sink.

Many oiled birds try to preen themselves, but the oil is too nasty for that; some don't give up the futile preening soon enough and die from swallowing oil that sticks in their bills. Even the most resourceful birds are completely helpless, and must sit and wait to die, with clogged nostrils and ears and eyes, unless they are lucky enough to be rescued by human beings.

Oil dumped quietly in a river doesn't attract much attention, and the birds it coats die in secret. But a coastal oil spill these days gets some press and draws a small number of professionals and volunteers who rescue waterfowl by taking them home and cleaning them. It is a long process, and each bird must be taken through it carefully: bathed with a mild detergent three times; fed frequently through a tube to stave off shock; and restored to buoyancy by stints of flotation over a period of several days. Many birds die from a combination of oil effects, shock, and too much handling. But some birds gradually recover the use of their feathers and return to the wild.

times conspicuous coloration, cunningly used, can save the life of a bird. A gaudy tail fully displayed by a bird being pursued from behind advertises itself as a handle, and may lure an overeager predator to come up with nothing but a claw full of feathers. When a dark junco fans its tail suddenly in the face of a threat, the flash of unexpected white feathers may bring an attacker up short for an instant—enough to mean the margin of survival for the small bird.

Obviously, conspicuous feather color does more than provide emergency flashes of defense. Above we said that feathers not only *do*, they *show*; now, we may add that feathers not only show, they *tell*.

For most human beings, the snap assessment that takes place when two people look at each other is so automatic as to pass unnoticed by the intellect. We would not admit to being a species dependent on visual display for our fundamental interests or fears. We think of communication as a conscious act of presentation and reception; words, expressing ideas that go deep, are what we believe we rely on. So it may seem strange to us that a couple of small beige slash marks on one small male brown bird's breast feathers are his most crucial communication to the world; if they are not pale enough to stand out well or if they are overgrown by adjacent feathers, he will not possess territory or breed; if they are bold he will be a star, owning great tracts of land and siring broods of little brown birds with even bolder beige marks year after year.

The decisiveness of such superficial things is not so strange, really. Could a white man from Nebraska meet a Chinese woman from Beijing and fail to notice her race and gender? Could a black man from London meet an aboriginal tribesman from Kalgoorlie and fail to notice his distinctions? Introduce a thirty-year-old Caucasian woman to two thirty-year-old Caucasian males of exactly the same height, build, and facial structure—but let one be a surfer from Malibu and the other a second-year student at the Harvard Business School. Will she notice any differences that incline her toward one or the other, at a glance? Of course. To pretend it isn't so is to belie our nature, and even our evolutionary trends.

Birds also depend on snap assessments. They have feathers, and they use them to communicate in a flash. When a male western kingbird lifts off from a fence post and shows the thin strips of white along the edge of his tail, he isn't just flying. He is saying, "Okay world, here I am, a western kingbird—not a Cassin's kingbird, as any fool can see by my tail, and not a tropical kingbird either; you wouldn't catch me dead with one of those gaudier red specks on my head. I live here, in this elegant little plot of land I'm showing you; I hope the smarter ladies among you will notice that it includes not only this stretch of grassland rich in insects but also access to that pond over there, and these four trees here, ideally placed for a warm little nest commanding a splendid view. In case you've been dozing, I'll fly around it again, showing those white feathers; they're really quite good ones. Okay. Any questions?"

When birds have odd feather configurations or wild colors for which no apparent function exists, chances are they serve a precise purpose in communicating important facts about identity, territory, sexual readiness, and competitive capability to other birds. We might see a cardinal and think, "What earthly good is a crest?" or a male lyrebird and wonder whether his crazy tail gets in the way. But a cardinal sees a cardinal and registers, "Okay—there's the crest, it's another cardinal, I guess this tree is taken," and a female lyrebird checks out that tail and responds, "Just what I've been looking for—a male lyrebird."

Most of the fancy plumage belongs to males because most of the competition for mates takes place between males. Sometimes they fight or at least pretend to, but much of the time they compete simply by strutting their stuff. Some species have reduced the mating game to a kind of Mr. Universe contest, in which the females of a colony gather around a tree or clearing that contains the males, who in turn line up and flex their feathers. The females evaluate the displays like judges at a body builders' contest, and make their selections.

As with feathers that aid in concealment, the display feathers are often used with a complementary action. Some acts are as quick and simple as raising neck feathers into a ruff; some are so long and intricate the bird may injure himself performing them, or at least exhaust his energy so that he needs time to recover before he can copulate with the mate his show has impressed. Quite aside from bodily movements such as hopping or whirling, the muscular control of the display feathers is very refined. It *has* to be, to execute some of the fancy plumesmanship. The peacock has some heavy feathers to whip around, as does the lyrebird—who fans them, shakes them one at a time in different directions,

The male argus pheasant unleashes its crest, tail, wings . . . but is the female in the foreground impressed?

Prince of the Waters

Ornithologists disagree about whether or not the uropygial gland is needed for waterproofing. Feathers *are* waterproof by their structure, and some waterfowl have small glands that barely function. The old-squaw duck dives 300 feet underwater, and is not especially oily. Yet experiments with other ducks have shown they ride lower and lower in the water when they go without their preening lubricant. It is probable that while the oil is crucial to some birds for repelling water, to others its use is primarily for keeping the beak from drying out or maintaining certain glossy feather colors.

One bird stands as a good argument for the waterproofing advocates. The dipper, or water ouzel, is probably the world's most aquatic bird, and it possesses a preen gland ten times larger than any other bird its size. It lives every minute of its life amid the splashes and sprays of Rocky Mountain rivers, flying in and out of waterfalls, nesting on the edge of white water, feeding on larvae in the mud of the river bottom—which it digs out during long strolls under many feet of icy water, like a towhee scratching for caterpillars on the floor of the forest. Yet the dipper is neither a duck nor a loon, gull, tern, plover, cormorant, or oyster catcher. It's "just another songbird."

If the shrike is a songbird that's really a hawk, the dipper is a songbird that's really a trout. Its capabilities underwater are amazing: on the bottom, it can hold its place in a river's crushing current for two or three minutes, bobbing cheerfully up in exactly the place it went down while a dabbling duck would have been carried a mile downstream. It can swim with or against the river at its own pace, using its wings as flippers. It has scratchy little songbird feet without webbing, so it rarely swims on the surface; instead, it has evolved retractable flaps to cover its nostrils, a sturdy nictitating membrane to protect its eyes, and that mammoth uropygial gland—all adaptations for use not *around* the water or *on* the water, but *under* it.

When it's not in the drink, the dipper behaves like a child who can't tear itself away from the ocean. It flies through sprays and waterfalls, singing joyously; it splashes

ripples them in unison, flattens them individually and together, and generally puts on a riot of coordination. The grouse has no special display feathers for his drumming routine, but the effort required to stand still on a log and beat the wings twenty times per second is as extraordinary as that exerted for any plume dance.

No matter what the action, however, nothing in a bird's use of a feather is more amazing than the feather itself. We come back to this, holding our found feather in our hand, with its 1 million interlocking parts, its prismatic color structure, its miracles of waterproofing and heat-trapping and air-cutting. We can look at it and say: If it weren't for this, there would be no birds. There is no comparable item determining the development of any other class of animal—no single unique possession, the subtraction of which from evolution would subtract the entire range of species who possess it.

The thing we hold in our hand seems even stranger when we consider that a short while

The dipper, in its element.

through shallows, bobbing its head 40 to 60 times a minute as if to keep the beat of the river's music; it stands on rocks and watches the water flow.

Dippers are very oily to the touch, and they bear a strong, musky smell. The uropygial oil obviously isn't used for buoyancy—floating isn't what a dipper wants to do. Instead, it slicks the feathers down and improves the bird's submarine design, keeping the water out at the same time. It may be waterproofing oil, but it's a different kind of waterproofing from that needed by ducks. In this way, the dipper is one more testament to a main principle of avian life: each species uses its common bird equipment for its own specific purposes. The equipment, remarkably, is versatile enough to serve.

ago it was a crucial part of a bird's body. We are not used to possessing discrete pieces of creatures that are still alive somewhere. The seashells we find on the beach are long-vacant houses of the dead; a bone or a shriveled snarl of fur in the woods is almost cruel evidence of an existence that has ceased. We don't get to touch the equipment of *living* wild animals. But when we hold a feather, there's a good chance the bird who lost it is winging along two counties to the south, quietly growing another million

parts to take its place. This is exciting, we are part of something. And it is fitting that our grasp of this excitement, the initiation of our bond with that bird away on the wing, is the small thing that gave the species its initiation long ago.

One summer evening my wife and I were eating dinner with some friends in a cottage on the rocky shore of a cove in Maine. There was a blue fog over the water, giving us the view of only a few feet of shallows where we were used to

The Flying Hydrant

Some of the most specialized feathers in the bird world line the belly of the male sand grouse. They are not hot pink display plumes, or spiky bristles for catching things; when dry, they look like normal ventral feathers, except that they are slightly furled.

Their specialty, however, is not being dry, but being *wet*—wetter, in fact, than any other feather on any other bird. The male sand grouse's belly feathers are designed to *hold* water so that the bird can transport it from water holes in its dry environment to the chicks who must have it to complement their dry diet of seeds.

The barbules along the shaft of the belly feathers are twisted in coils when dry. When the bird settles its belly into water (after rubbing it in sand to remove preening oil), the barbules swell into dense straightness, creating a spongelike texture that can hold water until the chicks drink from it.

seeing miles of ocean starting with the rocks twenty feet from our window. Because of this closing-in, on this evening we were not looking out as attentively as we usually did in the hopes of seeing osprey or eagles high in the distance. But at one moment, I happened to look out, and there, lean and tall even in his stooped hunting posture, was a great blue heron.

We gathered around the window and watched for almost half an hour as he waded through our shallows, snatching fish from the water by shooting his pointed beak at them like an arrow. No one spoke. We noticed the relaxed droop of his twig toes when he pulled them out of the water for another step with his hinged-stick legs. We noticed how he drew his stomach in once he sighted a fish and pulled his tail up until his belly was almost parallel to the surface of the water. We all sucked in our bellies, too, and held our breaths, until from a tightly muscled pause he sprang into a full stretch and nailed another fish. He never missed a fish, and we never missed a motion.

Finally, he seemed to sigh, lift his focus from the water, and then lift his body from our rocks with a soft heave of broad fog-colored wings. In an instant—two wing beats—he had vanished. We stared at the unbroken fog. We looked at each other in the silence, and the same thought passed among us: Had we really experienced that?

The others moved to another room, chatting about a new subject. I went outside and walked down the wet rocks to the edge of the water. It was very quiet. The edge of the fog seemed to be within the reach of my hand on all sides; I was in a perfect closet of clarity, with just enough water, rocks, and air. Was this really the same space a great blue heron had occupied thirty seconds ago?

I looked at the water; *I* saw no fish. I looked at the fog. It showed no evidence of the bird's having cleaved it. I listened; there were no fading swishes of wings in the wet air. I felt a flicker of doubt. Not doubt that I had seen the bird, but doubt that the experience of being near him could be so intimate and natural and true. Where was the the wild bird now? I turned back toward the house. As I did so, I looked down at the curve of rocks on the edge of the water. There, staunch and dry, its downy parts fluffing in the breeze, was a bluish feather. I picked it up.

Contrasting patterns are demarcated by precise lines.

Sky Life

It is so easy to think of flight as one simple act. A bird on a branch lifts sudden wings, leans into the wind, and lets go. It's aloft, and it looks so natural up there.

It *is* natural up there. A bird in flight is destiny in motion—a creature using every iota of equipment and instinct put together for it by centuries of evolution. But flight is far from simple, and far from being "one movement." For a bird, flight is more like the sum of *all* things, a miraculous capability that takes everything a bird's got. Each body system has to do its part, each feature of physiognomy has to cooperate. If a bird had teeth instead of a beak, it couldn't fly; if its blood didn't kick in with more red corpuscles per ounce than any other creature in the world, it would never get off the ground. Almost any quirk we might question in avian physiology—Why such a zippy metabolism? Why feathers?—has its raison d'être in some esoteric requirement of flight.

On the ground, looking up, we cannot see the red corpuscles and hinged ribs making their complex contributions. We see a sleek, strange form doing something that goes against our own experience of the laws of nature, and doing it with unconscious grace.

Consider this: gravity is the most consistent element of human experience. We know it better than we know our comparatively periodic heartbeat or breath because there is not an instant when we do not feel its pull. Gravity *is* always the same, wherever we go, and for every person. We honor our Mikhail Baryshnikovs and Michael Jordans by saying they defy gravity when they leap a little higher than others and look light about it—but what is their defiance compared to the merest flutter of a wren?

So we tend to look at flight as a single act revoking this single law. But of course flight is not an escape from gravity; the bird in the air feels the pull as much as we do on the ground. In fact, as we shall see, the bird *uses* gravity to maintain its flight speed, much as we do when we coast on a bicycle down a hilly street. Gravity, to birds, is just one component to be combined

Facing page: Snowy owl.

Flamingos turn from long-limbed sprinters into flying splinters.

with everything else for the purpose of keeping aloft.

Kenneth Dial, a zoologist at Harvard University and the University of Montana, says a lot with the comment: "A bird in flight is truly poetry in motion, certain aspects of which are counterintuitive. For example, the major upstroke muscle (supracoracoideus), which lifts the wing toward the bird's back, is located on the bird's belly! Also, it's interesting that a single muscle (pectoralis major) is primarily responsible for powering, and possibly controlling, the position of the wing during downstroke. One would expect a suite of muscles to be responsible for this chore."

Dial and a team in the laboratories of two anatomists, G. E. Goslow, Jr. (Northern Arizona University) and F. A. Jenkins, Jr. (Harvard University), have been getting the first "inside" look at how a bird's body stays in the air by shooting high-speed movie X-ray film of starlings flying in a specially designed wind tunnel. Before this, students of flight have had to watch a bird fly within a body mask, as it were, of feathers. If they wanted to look at bones and ligaments and things, the scientists had to use a dead specimen for dissection.

"A dead bird can only shed light on the structure of the apparatus used for flight, but it limits one's ability to understand how the equipment works," Dial says. "When you are confronted with a lifeless form you're restricted in deter-

Most birds flap themselves off perches; they rarely leap. (Atlantic puffin, Swainson's hawk)

mining just how the components behave and interact. One is tempted to draw conclusions about avian locomotion from the anatomy alone. While dissection represents the initial and an important stage within the field of functional anatomy, we should be encouraged to look further. Understanding precisely when the nerves fire to activate muscles responsible for the coordinated expansion and contraction of the elaborately designed avian wing has been the logical line of research to follow descriptive dissection."

Dial emphasizes that flight is a dynamic process requiring complex interactions among the nerves, muscles, tendons, bones, and feathers. Monitoring the living animal is opening new and exciting channels of discovery and addressing questions about flight unknown before.

The X-ray films (combined with a record of the electrical impulses sent from the nervous system to flight muscles) present us with a novel view of flight. For the first time we are viewing the internal dynamics of the bird on the wing plus the analytical insight beyond the feathers. Dial is quick to point out that 16-mm "home movies" of a few starlings hardly stand as comprehensive, revolutionary research; their X-ray movies simply indicate new and innovative ways

of thinking about how the bird's systems work in concert to put it in the air.

Home movies or not, the inside look provides some surprises—birds fly with their arm bones more acutely bent inside the extended wing than is usually appreciated; the neural control of the massive pectoralis muscle does not entail a single, large electrical surge as generally thought, but rather a complex series of impulses that allow the single muscle to operate as several individual muscles. Bones such as the sternum and clavicle contribute very lively action to the process, sometimes even leading the muscles into a contraction or expansion rather than just sitting like a static frame upon which the dynamic muscles are hung.

There are other anatomical revelations gained by the X-ray view, but perhaps what is most surprising about them is that they hold surprises at all. Man has been studying bird flight with wonder, envy, and calculation for many centuries. We have created ingenious technologies to assess and manipulate everything from the tiniest physiological functions of man and beast to the grand forces of hurricanes and avalanches. We can sponsor or repress populations of almost any kind of life—at our whim and often in our

Uses of Flight—Speed

Flight is the fastest way of getting around. The speediest ground animal, the cheetah, can sprint for short distances up to 70 mph. This wouldn't even get him into a qualifying heat in a sky race: many birds can accelerate past the 100-mph barrier, and some—certain swifts, doves, falcons, and sandpipers—approach 200 mph.

Speed has its obvious uses in escape from danger and migratory travel. It's good for the elemental requirements of survival, too: if your caloric reserves are ticking away on your internal clock and you have a lot of ground to cover in the search for food, you can cover it faster on the wing. A hawk can methodically examine a huge field in swift passes up and down its length; an albatross can crisscross vast surfaces of the sea in fast, long dives.

Once the hawk spots its prey, it can zip in for the kill in about the amount of time it takes to say "proceed with dispatch and terminate." Speed always surprises slower creatures. A hare can never truly adjust to the fact that a hawk way up in the sky can be on its back in a second or two; by the time the bird's presence registers, it's too late.

The swiftest kill in the world is the work of the falcon—so is the swiftest measured flight. In one of ornithology's most famous sightings, a peregrine falcon intently whizzed past an airplane doing 175 mph. The peregrine is a perfect representative of the falcons—very fast fliers with a daunting desire for the very quickest prey: birds, most of them caught in full flight.

The challenge of chasing birds demands terrific versatility as well as speed from falcons. Basically they are flapping fliers, whipping along with rapid, shallow beats of their thin, curved wings. They can also glide and soar well, straightening the wings and fanning the pointed tips to a rounded edge while their long tails spread into a diamond shape. But their virtuosity doesn't stop with mastery of these two main flight styles. The kestrel, smallest of the falcons and least given to eating birds, hunts most frequently from a fluttery hover, looking over the ground. The merlin, which eats almost nothing but birds, kills and eats on the wing. A merlin will mimic the generic flap-and-glide flight of songbirds to insinuate itself into the midst of a flock; once the finches or starlings realize who's among them, it's too late for all to scatter safely away. Sometimes the merlin drives a small bird up to dizzying heights and waits below until the exhausted prey has to coast down again. All falcons, especially those who prefer the "tail chase," can make dazzling changes of direction at full speed to follow the maneuvers of their prey or to execute aerial strategies of their own.

The most fearsome style of speed belongs to the peregrine. It prefers to hunt from a vast height, gliding 1,000 feet or more above the earth, watching for an unwary bird to pass far beneath it. The peregrine has picked a pretty challenging bird for its favorite prey—the pigeon, which itself is capable of flying 100 mph.

If a pigeon appears beneath the peregrine, the raptor waits until the prey is in the open, at the farthest point from shelter among trees. Then it performs one of nature's most terrifying feats (with one of man's most inappropriate-sounding names): *stoop-*

Wings against wings: a goshawk catches a hooded merganser.

ing. The stoop is a propelled free-fall from on high, in which the falcon becomes a bullet with wings tucked to its sides, flaring just enough to guide in the chase. The speed is defiant. Sheer gravity cannot match it; nor can any device in the natural world. Certainly the otherwise fleet pigeon cannot: before it can feint or dash away the peregrine hits it feetfirst with a colossal wallop, breaking its back and spraying its feathers in a puff like a down pillow burst in a kids' bedroom fight.

laboratories. We have even invented a flight of our own—indeed, our ability to take fantastic machinery far beyond the skies roamed by mere birds is often cited as mankind's most sophisticated achievement.

Yet we have never really figured out how the bird on that fence post over there flies to this fence post over here. The answer, obviously, does not lie in the field of measurement and calculation; neither can it be found in observation or imitation. (It is only when men stopped trying to fly the way they thought birds did that they got off the ground.) To scientists committed to some ideal of absolute comprehension, it must be frustrating to face the mystery. But to the rest of us, there is something marvelous in the unsolvable nature of bird flight. It soars above our ability to understand, as surely as a peregrine soars above our ability to see. To us this is fitting. Flight, we feel from our earthbound souls, *should* be free—from the encirclement of science as well as from the nagging of gravity. It is enough to watch, and to know that birds can do it because they are birds—everything about them makes it so.

Design

If we set out to design a flying creature, we would evolve a list of clear requirements; later, we would need to create mechanics that met them.

1. *Lightness.* The more that we give gravity to hold, the harder its bondage will be to break. We need to keep our creature's weight as low as possible; every milligram that can be cut must go.

Most earthbound creatures have no need to place such an emphasis on keeping trim. The hippopotamus is not punished by nature for being portly, and the skink is not especially favored for being svelte. Of course, weight is not a random matter for these creatures: every animal tends to find a weight that sustains strength and maintains body temperature without restricting its ability to move with whatever agility is needed to hunt, flee, forage, play, or compete for a mate. But most mammals have a larger margin for error than our fliers. A polar bear with an extra ten pounds of fat is not going to wake up one morning unable to walk. A flying creature who puts on a couple of ounces might have more trouble.

This snowy owl has just started its upstroke.

Some ducks run along the water to take off; others, such as this pintail, burst upward with one powerful snap of the wings.

2. *Power.* Flight will take a lot of work. Our creature needs lots of energy and strength, but *not* from the usual sources of rich fat, bulky muscle, and thick bone.

3. *Streamlined equipment for propulsion and control.* Air won't let our creature push off or grip or scull, quite unlike a foot on earth, a tire on macadam, or a fin in water.

A means of strong propulsion must be devised—if possible, one that takes *advantage* of air's relative slightness. The same should hold true for the means of control: the vague surfaces of air should be used for a new directive flexibility.

Air may be slight, but after all, it is *not* an abstract concept of nothingness. It is *matter,* with volume and density. It resists penetration, albeit less stoutly than solids and liquids.

A flying creature needs to move through the air with minimal friction. This means being sleek, even with all of its propulsive devices. It also means having a kind of *adjustable* sleekness, capable of responding to currents that can come from any angle while the bird is trying to proceed forward. Air is hardly a static medium; ask the skipper of any sailboat. Its density is variable, too—flying through moist air over the Florida Everglades takes a different kind of thrust than flying over Arizona's Sonora Desert.

To meet these requirements is quite a task,

Uses of Flight—Play

If birds didn't play, they'd be missing a good thing. Human beings spend a lot of time trying to get off the ground for new heights of amusement—whether it's flying in fast planes, hang gliding off mountains, skydiving, or just doing a one-and-a-half jackknife dive off the high board at the pool. To think that a bird, blessed with the ability to whip around the sky at will, would fail to amuse itself is an affront to our well-developed idea of play.

Certain birds seem to be playing in flight all the time, seizing tiny instants to exhibit a flourish or a feint, in between catching one food item and the next. All swallows, for example, act like nine-year-olds just let out of an overheated classroom for recess. They wheel and swoop and dip and dive over the surface of a pond with obvious exuberance. Sure, they're gathering food by cutting cleverly through shifting crowds of insects—but no one can convince us they're not jazzing it up for kicks.

Many birds, however, seem utterly sober about flight, with good reason. It takes a lot of energy, which birds are ill-equipped to waste. There are important things to do while in flight: find food, escape predators, patrol and defend territory, locate nesting sites and materials, migrate. Even impressing a would-be mate by performing aerobatic routines worthy of Olympic gymnasts is an act too desperately driven to be much fun. For the male bird, the evolutionary urge to propagate is behind every free-fall and somersault. Evolutionary urges just aren't the same as messing around with a few pals.

However, birds *do* mess around. One doesn't catch them at it as often as one sees them hunt or escape; therefore, we have no idea how regular the urge is, or how important. We also don't know all of the signs of play. Appearances can be deceiving—a chickadee may be working with grim fervor and look frolicsome while a condor might go through the aerial equivalent of disco dancing and we would interpret it as an act of composed majesty.

Ravens are certainly among the birds from whom we would expect very little playfulness. They are big, and definitively black. They eat carrion and they croak. Nothing lighthearted or zippy about them. Yet in the western United States, ravens are known for their frequent play in flight, especially through a maneuver known as

calling for new solutions to old needs most animals have long solved in ways that are fairly similar from species to species throughout the world. Very powerful animals are common enough: whales, elephants, bears, apes, sharks, tigers, and so on down the list of nature's big guys. But how do we generate and sustain great power without putting weight behind it? As for speed—cheetahs are quick, and so are bass, but they wear out after brief spurts. That's the way it is; most fleet creatures have traded endurance for speed. We don't want such a swap. We don't want to go to all the trouble of creating a flier just to have it come back to earth, exhausted, after 100 yards in the air.

So, our list contains three things that are al-

rolling. Ravens are very deft fliers, and one way they show it is by tucking their wings and rolling onto their backs for about a second in full flight, then rolling neatly back to an upright position. They don't do this in any pattern, or for any apparent reason—but they do it often. In some field studies, 20 percent of the ravens observed in flight performed some kind of roll—either the "half-roll" described above, a "full roll," in which the bird pauses for the upside-down second, then continues to roll in the same direction until it is upright, or a "double roll," in which two rotations are completed in a sequence. Some especially daring birds rolled onto their backs, then flipped along the tail-to-beak axis to wind up flying suddenly in the other direction, rather like a racing swimmer executing a kick turn against the end of the pool.

Ornithologists have tried everything to explain the raven's roll. Is it a courtship display? Probably not, as it occurs no more frequently in the spring than at non-mating times. Is it a form of social communication? Solo fliers do it as much as birds in a group. It is not accompanied by a vocalization or a response to a visible exterior stimulus. It does not occur only over certain topographical features of the land below. It has nothing to do with food, escape, or defense. It seems simply to be playful. The raven up there feels good and shows it in a joyous maneuver.

Another unexpected romper is the bald eagle. Play isn't usually associated with this bird, not only because of its size and dignity, but also because it is not known as an especially good flier. Yet eagles play in full flight, using ravenlike rolls, free-falls, mock strikes at other birds, and huge, wheeling dives. The eagle's play does seem to have a purpose—instruction in flight technique, whereby adult eagles channel the exuberance of juveniles into a kind of summer-camp lesson. Two adults will fly with three or four birds aged between one and three years (as determined by the solid brown plumage) in a loose formation. One adult will suddenly tuck into a roll, slip beneath a surprised youngster, and scrape its belly with a few rakes of the claws; then the adult turns right side up and swoops back into formation. Sometimes the upside-down attack ends in a sudden backward plummet for 100 feet or so. In any case, the kids soon get the idea and begin attacking each other upside down, sideways, or, as they gain capability and excitement, side by side in free-fall. The adults flap along, perhaps smiling to themselves as the minutes and maneuvers go by.

most mutually exclusive in the normal scheme of animal qualities. Obviously, to design the bird requires going far beyond the normal scheme. One of the beauties of the way the bird has evolved to fly is the fact that each requirement has not been met by a single feature—each need has been covered by numerous *layers* of features.

Lightness

Let's start with bones. Even in mammals, bones are built to be relatively light; nature *could* have endowed us with steel rods to serve their support functions. When we lift a forearm, we don't feel that the core of the limb is a heavy, stiff strut. It isn't—the mammalian skeletal system is a masterpiece of light strength, taking up just a small percentage of body weight.

Nevertheless, birds have cut a lot of weight from the skeleton, compared to other animals. They have done so in two ways: the construction of the bones from tissue and the arrangement of the bones in the body. Most bird bones are hollow. But they are not empty: where we have moist, heavy marrow, the bird has air sacs connected to the respiratory system, like an interior system of flotation balloons. The sacs penetrate deep, into narrow bones as well as spacious ones. For example, the hornbill's *toes* are pneumatically lined. The air sacs serve several purposes, including ventilation to help the bird cool itself, but the main one seems to be aiding aerial buoyancy.

The air sacs also give some interior support to the thin, hollow bones, which otherwise would be much like brittle straws—easily snapped. Even so, some of the larger bones, especially those in the wing and leg that bear the bird's weight in the air and on the ground, require stronger support. They get it from interior struts that crisscross geometrically, turning the brittle straw into a strong, rigid truss. Designers of roof supports and airplane wings came up with this simple buttress on their own—but it seems the bird beat them to it by several millennia.

The heaviest bone aggregate in any creature's body is the skull. There's a good reason: a lot of important stuff resides in the head. The brain is the only organ that seems to require protective bone enclosure in every animal (by comparison, the lungs are only loosely looped by the ribs), and its sensitivity demands a particularly thick plating. Eyeballs, olfactory organs, and ears usually take at least partial shelter in the skull. The mouth is contained in or extended from the skull, and has a bone network of its own—usually a heavy one, with jawbones capable of a powerful crushing action and teeth capable of desiccating tough food.

Birds need to cut down their skull weight. They don't do it by alleviating the skull's protective responsibilities—avian ears aren't shifted to the elbows or wing tips, and brains aren't reduced to tough little beads. On the contrary, birds have very large brains compared with other animals, and though their sense of smell is cut back, the need for superb vision means a larger eye apparatus, which makes up for whatever weight is saved by reducing olfactory organs. Hearing, too, is very sophisticated.

So the skull is packed and pressured. Like other burdened bird bones, the skull is constructed with crisscross struts, gaining strength despite a relatively thin surface. But it is in the construction of the mouth—or, rather, the transformation of it—that the bird saves a huge amount of weight over mammals and other creatures. Instead of a jawbone and teeth (the heaviest parts of the skull), the bird has a brittle, tough beak made of light bone covered with layers of horn. The beak bone is actually an extension of the skull, eliminating the need for heavily sealed joints (no tooth roots wrapping around a jawbone).

Many birds save some glandular poundage as well, by reducing salivary functions in the mouth, and moving some of them—enzymatic breakdown of food, for example—to the pharynx or another organ farther down the digestive tract. Saliva is for moisture alone; seed eaters have a lot, but birds with slippery diets (the heron, who eats lots of frogs; the toucan, who eats fruit) have lost most of their salivary glands. Pigeons have soft mouths inside their beaks, but most birds have tough interiors, with horny tongues and small, spikelike protrusions, used for crushing such food as seeds or insects. Birds don't really chew. But then, many animals with teeth don't chew either—the wolf tears chunks of meat from its prey and gulps them unmasticated in a bolt no less crude than that of the owl or pelican.

The beak is the most noticeable of several weight-trimming adaptations of the bird skeleton, but the others are just as revolutionary in the move from ambulation to flight. Most of them involve the fusion of bones or the creation of new sort of megabones—girdles that eliminate the need for certain joints.

The downstroke is a forward motion of the wings, not a backward push, as in the rowing of a boat. (golden eagle)

Joints are heavy; bones are knobby where they join, reinforced to withstand the pressure of motion and broadened to allow the attachments of the ligaments and cartilage that direct and cushion the torsion. The heaviest mammal joints are usually the hips—not surprising in an ambulatory creature whose walk pivots at or just below the center of gravity. Birds walk, too, but of course they prefer to fly—so they've evolved a broad pelvic girdle that reduces the weight of the skeletal apparatus for taking steps, while broadly distributing the burden of body weight from the scrawny legs to the back, *above* the center of gravity.

Most of the vertebrae in the bird's back and tail are fused. This creates a severe rigidity, limiting the bird's ability to rotate along the axis of its spine, but greatly increasing its strength and precision as a flier. Anyone who has tried to swim in a straight line knows that the spine's tendency to twist with the alternating extension of the arms creates a side-to-side motion that skews forward progress. Birds are better equipped to follow a line than we are. Their enforced straightness of spine keeps them more easily on line when they fly. And because the fused vertebrae essentially make the back a rod from which the rest of the bird hangs earthward, the pull of gravity on the body *reinforces* the adherence to line—rather like the keel of a ship.

Birds also have an actual keel, a blade in the center of the sternum that projects forward as clearly as the skeg on a surfboard. The bird's blade is so loaded with muscle, however, that it doesn't protrude beyond the contour of the body; in fact, its purpose is to provide a fastening place for the bird's extraordinary pectoralis—the breast muscle that drives the wings and makes up as much as 35 percent of the bird's entire weight. The special sternum is a strong but light plate, weighing far less than the complicated arrangement of cartilage and ligaments that would hold the pectoralis in a more conventional linkage with a flat breastbone and ribs.

The bird's ribbon-thin ribs are thus somewhat freer to move than in most animals. But ribs aren't exactly what we think of as dynamic body parts; we've seen so many skeletons with those brittle strips lined up like cages, the most passive

The breastbone is indeed a keel.

and inert kind of protection for lungs and heart. Why bother to liberate them? In fact, it goes even beyond liberation—to revolution. The ribs are one of only two spots in which joints have been *added* to the bird instead of removed. The joints are hinges that allow the outer third of each rib to jackknife inward during the downstroke of the wing as the sternum moves significantly inward to the body, against them. This motion—or series of motions—is clear in the Harvard film.

At first this would seem to be so perfectly in line with the compressive effects beating wings would have on the thorax that we *could* see the hinges simply as a device for accommodating that compression. The sternum's upward motion could be seen in the same way; that is, as a passive skeletal response to muscular initiative.

But the X-ray films suggest another possibility —that the skeleton of the flying bird is not the passive scaffolding we usually imagine bones to be, but a flexible, lively mechanism. The bellows action of the ribs and sternum appear to compress air sacs intimately associated with the lungs, which exhale during the wing's downstroke and draw the lower edge of the body into a tighter aerodynamic shape for the powerless instant between downstroke and upstroke—a tiny but essential adjustment. The movement of other bones, especially the clavicle, supports the idea that the skeletal structure, while it may not lead the muscles, is at least an active partner in certain motions.

This, in fact, plays a role in keeping weight down. As each movement of the bird in flight is necessary for its success, some body part makes the movement possible. Body parts have weight; remember our dictum that each part has to contribute—literally to pull its own weight. We cannot afford the luxury of a passive skeleton loaded with muscles and tendons that take all of the action. We need to make some use of the bones—give the ribs some responsibility and perhaps eliminate the need for a couple of ligaments; turn the clavicles into a spring and allow the reduction of the pectoralis by a few percentage points of mass. If the bird has to have bones, it might as well *use* them—to house air sacs, to contribute little motions complementing muscles, to distribute weight and rigidity along the flight lines.

Bones, of course, are only the beginning of the lightness. The skin covering those bones has its weight-saving qualities, too. Bird skin is very thin, and it contains no secretory glands, except for the uropygial gland at the base of the tail. Lots of glands make for a heavy epidermis. The most common gland in most mammals' skin—the sweat gland—is absent entirely: birds don't perspire. They cool themselves by flattening their feathers to squeeze heat away from the skin, and by using the air sacs that penetrate their body cavities for a complicated sort of interior ventilation. Again, each item serves multiple purposes in the cause of lightness.

Instead of a layer thick with glands and follicles, the outer surface of the bird's epidermis is composed of flattened epithelial cells. The speciality of these cells is the production of keratin, which creates the extremely light but strong feathers, claws, scales, and beak covering. The dermis underneath contains blood vessels and nerves for the bird's smooth muscles, which control the movement of feathers through the skin. Thus the skin is tight against the muscle, without the subcutaneous layers of vascular networks and fat that other animals carry.

Birds are as lean as nails. Dissecting a plump-looking robin beside a slinky weasel is a lesson in invisible leanness. Beneath the weasel's plush fur is the thick skin that anchors it, and beneath that is a generous filling of fat. The eelish contour doesn't tell the whole story; the weasel is in fact a heavy creature. The jocund robin's seeming plumpness is just as much a sham: beneath the puffy feathers lies a taut torpedo of a body, inside which one finds no more than a globule or two of adipose tissue. Almost everywhere the skin peels back from muscle without a speck of fatty interstice.

Birds' metabolic madness (a songbird's normal body temperature might be 108°, with a heart rate on the wing of 700 beats per minute)

Kestrels hover in the wind and drop sharply on prey.

doesn't give their bodies the chance to store much in the way of fat. Exceptions are before a molt (when loss of feathers inhibits the hunt for food) or a migration (when some birds actually fast for weeks while flying thousands of miles). Birds eat calorie-rich foods and burn them up fast with a digestive system that efficiently supplies their high-voltage metabolisms' demands. This has much to do with the power requirement (which will be examined in more detail later); but in terms of weight, an efficient digestive tract means a bird doesn't carry a lot of half-digested bulk or unjettisoned waste around in its intestines.

Uses of Flight—Instruction

Ornithologists disagree about how much adult birds teach their offspring to fly. The majority feel there is no instruction. Flight, they say, is such a natural activity for the bird, serving as the basis for nearly all of the instinctive survival behaviors, that it must be a completely innate ability. Birds just do it, they don't need to learn how. These skeptics feel it would be inconceivable for a creature to master the amount of technical instruction necessary for any of a thousand aerial feats. Who could learn how to change direction in 1/70 of a second when a gun goes off 150 yards away? Who could be taught to spread the two outer tail feathers an extra millimeter when a whiffle of crosscurrent alters the landing path in the last $\frac{1}{10}$ of a second before touchdown? Only spontaneous wisdom could inform such adjustments.

Other scientists insist that birds, like most other creatures, need to learn the subtleties from their experienced elders. There is not a lot of evidence of such instruction; in fact, many more fledglings have been seen learning the hard way—by falling out of the nest and facing the choice of flight or death. Sand martins, for example, often build their nests in the crevices of bridges, high above the surface of river or bay. The young stay in the nest until the fateful day they tumble out and either learn to fly in slightly less than two seconds *or* crash to a watery death in slightly more. Most of them fly, of course, or the species would be long extinct.

Believers in flight school say we shouldn't conclude that instruction doesn't occur just because we don't see it; there are a lot of things we don't see birds do. And there are several species well-known for their flight-training methods. Swallows, perhaps the most adroit fliers, use the exchange of food as the inspiration for learning. The kids begin by taking practice flights and being fed on the nest. Next, they are fed by the parents *only* as they fly, from beak to beak. Then the parents drop slain insects from

One-two, one-two. A nearly fledged bald eagle practices his strokes with his back to the still-fearsome sky.

Flying well takes practice. This young great horned owl came a cropper against a tree, but eventually righted itself and flew off.

farther and farther away, forcing the hungry fliers to catch their dinner. Finally, the young swallows go after living prey themselves. Observers have reported similar behavior among hawks.

This kind of coaching may seem to be more about hunting than pure flying. But the point is that *hunting* is about pure flying; so is almost everything the bird does. Any lesson an adult teaches a fledgling necessarily includes some instruction in flight.

Classes in aerial mechanics, unassociated with food, are not often witnessed. One summer on Chappaquiddick Island in Massachusetts, I was lucky enough to stumble upon a summer camp for young terns. Every morning for a week I sat on the beach and watched half a dozen adults lead a flock of perhaps twenty young birds into the air over a large, shallow tidal pond. The flock of students would hover, facing the crew of adults a little apart from them like gym teachers leading jumping jacks. Then the adults would peel off in dives toward the surface of the water. The first few dives on the first couple of days were greeted with confused chatter from the young birds. Repeated examples finally induced them to try the dives themselves, and soon the whole class was pitching earthward from a hovering start. The dives were messy at first, but after a while the fledglings became skilled at tucking, rolling, and dashing toward the surface of the water.

The adults soon changed the lesson: now, instead of diving from a hover, the birds were encouraged to dive from a slow forward flight. The tern's dive is not a direct plummet like the gannet's or pelican's; instead, there is a fine little transitional moment, a stutter step between the momentum of horizontal flight and the vertical propulsion toward the water. This transition is what the terns had learned first, and now that they had it down, they picked up the dive from full flight in no time.

(continued)

They still were not hitting the water—the dives had only taken them to within a foot or so of the surface. To my surprise, however, the youngsters showed no hesitation after the adults showed them the way into and out of the water. It was as if the young terns saw the logical sequence of their instruction and wanted to make full use of what they had learned so far. The students handled the difficulties of the water very well.

The tern's immersion is one of the weirdest sights in nature. The flying bird hovers for an instant, snaps downward, and hits headfirst with a splash, all of which seems fairly normal—but then there is a very odd moment, when the tern pulls up on the surface, jerks its wings into a half-flex, and freezes. Watching the checked moment, one feels the world absolutely stop. The very shape of the splash around the rising bird registers as a still life of bubbles and droplets. Major forces seem to hang fire, as though gravity were defied. Then, like a movie shown by a chattering projector, the scene jumps back to life. The bird completes its wing beat and rises straight up, the laws of nature intact.

It took very few dives before the young birds mastered this hesitation move. They splashed and rose in the pond many times, chirping in satisfaction with themselves. The adults circled above them, and finally led them home.

The next day's lesson was the final one. All that changed was the water, for instead of the pond the trainees were ushered out over the Atlantic. There they were led through their paces once again, the adults flying and hovering and diving and rising as examples. Several times a young tern pulled out of a dive as it neared the choppy surface; but eventually all of the birds attacked the sea as they had the shallow tidal pool. This led to much celebration and raucousness; indeed, the flight became as sloppy as it had been the first day, during the initial dives. The difference was that now it seemed a conscious mockery of an earlier stage. It was bad grammar at graduation, a ballet student pretending to trip after taking bows at a recital.

The next morning I came back at the same time, but I suspected I would see no tern class. I was right. A few birds flew by, out over the sea. They flapped and dove. But I could no longer tell the students from the teachers.

Food not immediately in use isn't the only thing the internal bird objects to hauling off the ground. It holds no truck with gonads and off-spring, too. The sexual organs of both sexes lie shriveled inside the abdomen, like wisps of freeze-dried lettuce, from fall to spring; only at the onset of breeding season, after the spring migration, do they come to life, swelling as much as 500 times their off-season mass. The urge to breed is thus a rather sudden compulsion—one minute a male sparrow has a couple of inert sand grains chafing his kidney, the next minute he has throbbing testes the size of ripe garden peas. Females have a single reproductive tract (one ovary and oviduct) instead of the double we find in many other animals. It produces an embryo they get rid of as fast as possible. Unlike viviparous mothers who bear the young inside through much of its prenatal development, the female bird coats the freshly fertilized zygote with a calcium shell and immediately squeezes it out into a nest. This can happen fast—in some species less than a day elapses from copulation to the laying of a fertile egg. No wonder a female won't entertain the male's advances until he has finished building her a comfy nest; the nursery had better be ready before the first amorous gleam in the eye is even acknowledged.

Power

We have noted that in most animals lightness and power are rarely products of the same features. The trim cheetah is a pretty awful killer for a big cat; although it can sprint nimbly with impalas, it is rather weak in the jaw and forelimbs. Its strapping cousin, the lion, can barely catch a lame gnu in an open field run, but it can pulverize the big antelope's vital parts with a snap of the jaws or a wrench of the wrists.

In the bird, however, power and lightness are miraculously affiliated. In fact, many of the features that make the bird light also make it strong; such is the ingenuity of avian evolution. Getting off the ground and staying there requires an immense generation of force, no matter how many air sacs a bird has or how delicate the ribs might be.

An animal gets power from food. Birds eat a lot—daily, they ingest food equal to a quarter of their body weight, or more. For an owl this may mean gulping a couple of voles; for a pine siskin it means extracting and pulping a few thousand thistle seeds. However, the owl usually has to spend more energy hunting and killing its prey than a siskin spends locating a thistle or cone. It is a perilous irony of bird life that birds need to fly to find enough of their food, while the reason they need so much food is to power their flight. Birds that survive have struck a balance between calories expended for food and calories gained for sustenance. The margin is usually very small.

Birds' digestive systems are voraciously efficient. They eat foods that produce high energy relative to bulk—nuts, seeds, insects, worms, fish, animals, and in the case of the hummingbird,

nectar that is almost pure sugar—and they get the most out of their diets fast. A young cedar waxwing swallows some fruit, softens it in the stomach, pulverizes it in the gizzard, sucks it clean of nutrients in the liver and intestinal tract, and evacuates the tiny unused matter, all within sixteen minutes. Most other birds aren't much slower, processing their food in less than two hours.

Haste does not make waste: relative to the volume of food they eat, birds excrete very little. Instead, they have an uncanny ability to turn their seeds and worms into muscle. A young bird can gain 1 kg of new body weight by eating just 3 kg of food. A young mammal, even on a similar diet, must eat 10 kg to gain the same amount.

Muscles get power from oxygen. Oxygen is delivered by blood, and here, too, the bird is exceptionally blessed—with a huge respiratory system and a booming heart that pumps blood high in sugar concentration. A duck's respiratory system takes up 20 percent of its volume, most of it in the air sacs (human lungs take up 5 percent). Those air sacs, aside from being buoyant bone filler, allow a vastly greater capacity for taking oxygen into the body and rushing it into the blood. Then the heart (comparably five times larger than a man's) pumps it ten times as rapidly through the whirring little body. Every bit of air is needed, not just for oxygen nourishment— the high temperature generated by this frantic metabolism requires an extra coolant, which the sacs provide. As much as 75 percent of the air that a bird takes in will be used only for cooling, through the sacs.

Birds have a complex system of muscles, many of them limited to very specific manipulations of feathers. But the main beneficiary of all of this power production is a single muscle—the pectoralis, attached to the sternum's keel on one end and the humerus (upper arm) on the other. The pectoralis pulls the wings through the downstroke in flight. This is the biggest job in the flying bird's body. Accordingly, the pectoralis is the biggest body part, taking up 30 to 50 percent of the bird's weight.

Uses of Flight—Territory

Birds move around the world a lot, but they are not nomads. Between migrations, they define and defend territory as rigorously as wolves. A male bird stakes out land to which he hopes to attract a female because it is rich in food, nesting sites, or shade. A community guards feeding grounds to protect their common resources of berries or bugs. Individuals and teams set boundaries beyond which predators must be driven. The territory may shift season by season for mating grounds, or even week by week in the case of food supplies; but it must be patrolled.

The first line of defense is a bird's song, which essentially means: Here I am, females welcome, males keep off. This doesn't scare everybody; it may even attract predators. So a bird has to patrol his territory. Obviously, flight is a great boon for reconnaissance and defense. Some aerial defense is passive. Many birds have dashing marks that show only when they fly; these serve as a posted warnings to others who see them. Sometimes a warning isn't enough and an intruder needs to be chased away to know the land-owner means business. A bird on the wing can spot a breach in its defenses from on high, chase another creature away, and return to the patrol, all very quickly.

In some cases of intrusion and defense, simple flight can become a deadly weapon. One winter morning I was riding along the edge of a remote Massachusetts beach with the caretaker of a huge wildlife refuge; we had been exploring his fiefdom for hours, lightly touching the down in empty eider nests and the fractured eggshells of egrets and herons, generally enjoying the evidence of birds' vitality through their detritus. It had been a silent day. Most of the birds whose effects we had found were far away by now—the only live ones we had seen were a few big eider ducks skimming the flashing sea to the north of our peninsula's tip.

We rode along a path through the salty grasses, with the straight white beach to our left, without speaking, and probably without expecting to see any wildlife: so far, the feathers and footprints had been enough. But all of a sudden we flushed a small brown bird from the dune between us and the sea. It shot from the grassy cover at a weird angle, its wings lifted in a V above its back. Obviously alarmed, it flapped and bobbed erratically over the beach. "Young owl," said my guide. Then to the bird he said: "Calm down, little fellow."

However, the owl showed no signs of calming down. It was startled; it was young; and it may not have been used to flying this early in the day. Surrounded by blinding sunlight reflected sharply from water and sand, it lost its bearings and flapped its stiff wings more and more frantically, moving slowly away from the dune it sought. The caretaker spoke again, this time with an edge of urgency to this voice: "Whoa, little fellow. Stay over the beach. Don't keep going, now. Don't get out over the water."

We watched. When it was clear that the owl was in fact going to stray out over the water, I asked why it was important that it avoid this. My guide just sighed as the owl fluttered—ever so slightly—past the invisible line demarking beach airspace from water airspace, and nodded: Watch.

Crows chase a female marsh hawk who strayed over their territory.

Three new birds appeared in the sky as if created on the spot by the owl's verge into the marine air. In fact, the birds—mature herring gulls—had been in the same dune grass from which the owl had sprung, and had watched its flight just as we had. The moment the owl broke the sky's seal between land and sea, they dashed into the air in a tight line, almost wing tip to wing tip, like a small squadron of fighter planes. They were facing the open sea. And they were flying, in a patient but determined way, right at the owl.

It saw them, flapped madly for another few moments; then, the familiarity of the gulls' threatening presence seemed to bring back some of the owl's senses. It righted itself, assumed a fairly regular wing beat, and flew in a straight line toward the edge of their formation, obviously intending to get its wayward self back where it belonged. For a moment, it looked as if all would be all right: as if it were saying, "Okay, guys, I get the message—sorry!" The gulls, silent and ghostly in their gray-and-white, would watch the owl return to its dune and then return to their own space.

But it was not to be. Just as the owl was nearing the edge of the formation, the gull in the middle peeled out of the line and flew farther out in its direction, establishing a new outer limit to the formation, and leaving the owl now in the middle. The new central gull—the former outside bird the owl had been about to scoot past—now pushed forward from the line with a pickup in speed and drove right at the owl. The owl, startled once more, veered off to one side and retreated in the only direction it could: back toward the sea. The middle gull did not let up in precise pursuit. It chased the owl, nose to tail, never quite catching up as the owl retreated and dodged. Behind the chasing gull, the other two kept formation, pushing the line farther and farther out from shore. Once the owl made a frantic feint in one direction, then burst furiously in another around his pursuer. But as soon as it came near the line established by the formation, the gull nearest him peeled out and assumed the pursuer's role. The original pursuer took its place in the formation. This changing of the guard happened a few times, until it was clear that the gulls were duping the owl into it, forcing it to burn up energy while they calmly replaced each other with a fresh gull.

(continued)

The line set by the patient, easy flapping of the gulls moved regularly out toward the horizon. Soon I could see only the four specks: two of them nearly immobile, two of them locked in a dance, but always getting farther from shore with every wing beat. I was horrified. "What are they doing to it?" I asked.

"Killing it," my host replied.

It didn't *look* like killing, though it certainly *felt* that way. "How?" I asked.

"They'll just keep driving the owl out to sea until it drops. And drowns. In a few days some fisherman will come up with its body and wonder what an owl is doing four miles offshore. Meanwhile these gulls will be back home. And it will be a long time before another owl in this area dares to go out over the water. See, that's the gulls' territory. The owls and hawks can hunt the land all they want, right up to the water's edge. But if they go one inch farther, they have to die."

"Wouldn't it be better to scare the bejesus out of it, and let it return to tell the tale?"

My host shrugged. "Other birds learn this way as well. And if you're into evolutionary theory, you could say only those birds instilled with fear of the air over the water will survive and pass it on."

I looked out. The dots were invisible now. I did not want to wait around for the cool, triumphant threesome to return silently home, leaving the exhausted little owl awash in the distance. "Let's go," I said. My host put the jeep in gear. As we were about to pull away, I realized something; what particularly bothered me about the owl's plight was that it was being killed with pure aloofness. There was no screeching and scrabbling, no flashing talons or slashing beak, no last hurrah as it hurled itself against three adversaries in a desperate physical challenge. The owl just got flown to death. The gulls turned the fact that it could fly against it, made it use its special ability to drive itself out of life. "They never touched the owl," I said. "It's just plain dishonorable."

"No, it's just plain smart," said the caretaker, as we drove on. "A gull doesn't have the physical weaponry to kill a *clam* 'honorably,' one on one. Webbed feet, a kind of a clunky bill, no speed, no agility. So it uses the one weapon it has. The gull carries clams up in the air and drops them onto rocks. It chases enemies out over the water. It turns the one thing it can do pretty well into a deadly force, once in a while."

"Flight," I said. "Pure flight as weapon." I sighed. "Somehow, I never think of it that way."

"Birds do," he said. "Ask the owl."

As with the bone girdles, where lots of complicated functions were transferred from many moving parts to a larger functional unit, the simple puissance of one big muscle probably saves weight and space. The Harvard X-ray team has published research showing that this whopper actually has very refined neurology behind it, so that instead of slamming the wing down in response to one huge electrical impulse, the pectoralis moves with smooth complexity. It has the advantages of a single muscle—power concentration and conservation, durability, simplicity of maintenance—without sacrificing the functional sophistication of a more complex structure.

Birds can improvise new maneuvers in flight by using each wing independently.

"Well," says Kenneth Dial, "you need some help if you're going to try something as demanding as flying."

Streamlined Equipment for Propulsion and Control

In evolutionary terms, birds did not grow wings; they "evolved specialized forelimbs." The creature that became the bird started with four feet, like any lizard or cat, and it walked on all of them. But in time the creature's descendants started rearing up on their hindlegs, perhaps to run after insects (or away from pursuers). Those who ran this way survived better than the four-footed trotters and passed on the bipedal inclination to their descendants. Gradually the body's center of gravity began to shift rearward to counterbalance the hoist of the front legs and head; the front legs, released from the job of bearing weight and running, started to develop a knack for reaching, grasping, even climbing.

Archeopteryx evidently ran on its back legs quite a bit, when not scrambling around in trees so that it could glide down again. Perhaps its first glide came at the end of a hard run after an insect just out of its reach when, instead of slowing down on its feet, it simply lifted them up and leaned forward, throwing its weight onto the air beneath the broadened surface of its wings. Probably it glided a few feet, comparable to the Wright brothers' first flight, and then landed on its belly; but the impact would have been worth it. The dinosaur had discovered quite a trick.

There are theorists who think Archeopteryx's feathered forelimbs evolved purely as a kind of insect net; the ancestral bird ran on its back legs and circled bugs in front with its wings, sweeping them toward its mouth. They don't say why Archeopteryx had feathers on its tail. But whatever the reason for the wings, we can see today what became their prime usage. Birds in our world use their wings for flying, and sometimes for swimming. Almost none have kept the inclination to reach for an object with the wing as if it were an arm, and the grasping fingers Archeopteryx retained on *its* wing were long ago subjected to the needs of flight, brought inside the skin of the wing proper. The lammergeier, a huge Eurasian vulture that attacks live prey, tries to knock animals down with great swats of its wings, and the young of the South American hoatzin, born with a couple of vestigial fingers, pulls itself up on tree branches with the temporary wing digits. Otherwise, if you put something in front of a bird that it wants to pick up, hit, or climb over, it reaches automatically with its beak or claw.

Because the evolutionary changes of the bird's forelimb have been so spectacularly successful, the previous form is hard for us to appreciate. When we watch a golden eagle in flight, we do not associate its gnarled, scaly legs with its vast, flat wings—we do not see it as a creature with

four roughly similar limbs. But for all of their distinctness, wings maintain much of the basic skeletal structure of the arm. Moving outward from the shoulder, we find a humerus, an elbow, a radius and ulna, a wrist, and digits. In general, these bones and joints have been altered a bit for the special movements of flight, especially the "fingers," which are reduced in number and fused at the joints; it could be said that these have become more of a hand bone from which the primary flight feathers project as the bird's functional fingers.

What is most surprising about the wing-*cum*-arm-*cum*-leg's adaptation to flight is not that nature has taken the liberty of fusing a couple of digit joints. It is that so *few* liberties have been taken with a basic structure for such a revolutionary activity. Flying is so different from walking or climbing: How can the structure

This red-tailed hawk shows that a bird is indeed a four-limbed creature with a torso—a shape we associate with mammals and many reptiles, but rarely with birds.

Uses of Flight—Escape

Birds have the ultimate ability to execute the second half of the fight-or-flight reaction, with which nearly all creatures respond to a sudden threat. Not surprisingly, most birds prefer to fly from trouble instead of standing ground and attacking (unless they are protecting a nest, are redwing blackbirds, or both). But even the most skittish creatures cannot match the bird's disappearing act: one instant it's there, and the next it's over the far hills into the next county.

For all of their flourish in fleeing, birds do not escape madly; nor do they go as far away as it seems they intend to. Watching them blaze into the sky at a speed of 70 mph and zip to dot size on the horizon, we might think they won't be back for a week, but in fact they return to their territory, albeit sneakily. Defense is never far from their intent.

Different families of birds have different strong points as fliers. Hawks are made to hunt, hummingbirds to hover. Pheasants, quails, chickens, grouse, turkeys, and woodcocks have an unusual specialty on the wing: they are made to *escape*.

These birds, which feed on the ground and if left undisturbed would probably walk forever, take to the air only when compelled to do so. They hide in thickets if someone comes creeping through the fields or woods, and fly only as a last resort for a quick getaway. This rather reticent attitude toward flight shows up in the physiology. For example, the escapers have the huge breast muscles of active fliers, but there is a difference any eater of game knows. Where the breast meat of a duck is dark because as an active muscle it receives a lot of blood flow, the more inert breast of the chicken or pheasant is whiter, because it is not so deeply infused with blood.

An escaper can take off like the proverbial bat from a hot place: from complete silence on the ground it explodes into the air with a loud, whacking rustle of feathers. The sound is alarming, and throws many a hunter backward for an instant—often the instant that lets the bird whirr into the safety of trees. Some pheasants actually produce a clap or bang as they snap their big wings into action and rise. This crack accompanied by the nearness of the sudden wild creature is unsettling.

The rise is immediate—no ducklike running start here—and so is the speed: the escaper is the drag racer of birds, whipping through the lower gears and reaching top velocity in a few seconds. But like the drag racer, the bird is made for the short sprint, burning too much fuel too fast to keep up the pace for more than 100 yards or so. If you can repeatedly flush and follow a grouse four or five times, you may finally be able to walk up to it and lift it in your hand—the bird will be too exhausted to get into the air again, until the meager network of blood vessels can nourish those breast muscles.

fundamental to each stay so similar? Across the full range of bird life—the largest class of animals in the world—there is amazingly little variation in the structure of the forelimb. The hummingbird's wing, although specialized for its unique flight style, has more in common with a condor's wing than does a human arm with that of its fellow mammal, the dolphin. Obviously, once evolution came up with the wing, it had a winner; so from species to species it followed that wise principle of nature: "If it ain't broke, don't fix it."

The secret of such consistency lies in the fact that the fundamentals of the wing include much more than the bone structure. The wing without the feather would be a wagon without the wheel. It is the flight feathers that turn the basic structure's crude aerodynamics into zippy streamlines, and that perform all of the actual body-meets-air miracles upon which flight depends. Wings covered with single sheets of light, strong vinyl would not do what bird wings do. Unlike mammalian bats, birds do not scull through the air, using their wings as if they were solid paddles pushing off a resistant surface.

We see a wing beat as a single action of the bird's largest body part, but really the big, simple stroke is just the means of putting the feathers into play. The primary feathers on the down-stroking wing tips twist against the air individually, with a rotating action very similar to that of propellers. They *screw* through the air, providing most of the forward thrust. Meanwhile, the other wing feathers are channeling the air that's passing above and below the wing so that lift is maintained and the force of gravity is used to help the *forward* momentum, not to pull the bird straight down.

Different kinds of flight require different wings, but all birds' blunt front edges do the same thing: cut the air into two streams. One zips rapidly over the top, due to the contour of the wing, and another passes slightly more slowly underneath. The slower stream rushes to match the speed of the faster, so they will meet at the rear of the wing in phase. This creates more air

pressure beneath the wing than on top, which lifts the wing.

Nature does not seem to like resistance to natural motion; whenever something can be shaped to smooth its passage through a medium (or a medium's passage around it), nature finds a way. When the medium is air, the perfect shape is easy to discover: we need only to drop some water.

Water is shapeless and heavy—just the right substance to register innocently the effects of air and gravity. If we drop a small amount of water from a high place, gravity and air turn it into the shape we call a teardrop, to reduce as much as possible its resistance to the pull and pressure. The thick curve of the leading edge cleaves the air along the sloping sides and off the tapered back edge. It's simple, elegant, and fast.

The teardrop shape is the aerodynamic theme of the bird. It's easy to see it repeated on different levels throughout the physiognomy. Because a bird travels more or less horizontally through the air, we need to turn the teardrop sideways. If we do so, we come up with the general outline of the flight feather, the wing, and the body.

Aerodynamics does not mean just the passive reduction of resistance, of course. As the name implies, it has active effects. The passage of air around the modified teardrop of the wing creates lift, while the passage around the primary feather creates propulsion. The body, led by the slicing beak, torpedoes its way along, channeling air to the tail so that this mechanism of control has something to work with.

Birds have evolved many of the streamlining adaptations that make aquatic mammals so sleek, but have taken them farther. Mammals evolving toward life in the water are losing (or at least reducing) their external ears, as such protuberances block the smooth flow of water over the head. Ears sticking out on a nuthatch would do the same, disrupting the neat curve of air flowing from beak to tail. So birds have their ears completely inside the body, with small orifices instead of the catchall shells we carry around.

Aquatic mammals tend to reduce long limbs that break up the flow of water around the body: the pinnipeds (seals, sea lions) have taken their skeletal arms inside the thorax until all that remains sticking outside the torpedo line of the skin is the hand, while swimmers such as the muskrat have shrunk their little-used forelimbs to twigs while increasing the size of the webbed rear feet that provide propulsion in the water. Birds, of course, have turned their protruding forelimbs into the means of aerial propulsion—but they have also made them aerodynamic, and provide for them to tuck neatly away, exactly fitting the contour of the body. The rear limbs have become twigs that are pulled up against the belly in flight and do not disturb the lines of airflow.

There is evidence that a sense of aerodynamics extends into behavior. An osprey that has caught a fish will not fly with it broadside to the wind, though this is the natural way to grab it from the water. Instead, the large hawk carefully grasps the fish with one foot in front of the other along the fish's spine, using its excellent aerodynamic design to complement the bird's own.

Penguins swim by flying underwater. Their only airborne moments come when they propel themselves out of the water into an upright landing.

Flightless

If flight is so great, why have some birds evolved away from it? Most ornithologists believe that at one time in its evolutionary history, each species of bird was capable of flight; yet today we have penguins, kiwis, ducks, rails, cormorants, grebes, emus, ostriches, cassowaries, rheas, owl parrots (kakapos), and—until it became extinct quite recently—even a wren that cannot fly. In addition there are several birds—the roadrunner, for example—who prefer to walk or run, even though they can fly adequately. If evolution is indeed always progressive, how could a bird lose the ability to fly and still be gaining in strength? And what about the recent extinction of several flightless species—the wren mentioned above, the great auk, the dodo, and others? Do these events argue that evolution might have messed up when it allowed birds to get accustomed to the ground?

Not really. We must remember that flight is not a free ride—it requires a tremendous expenditure of energy. A bird should spend that energy only if it is required to do so for survival. If it flies when it *could* be walking, in the long run it will very likely fade away like a burned-out rocket falling over the horizon.

If we look at flightless birds we can see in each case that they simply lost the need to fly. Evolution operates its dispensation of special abilities much like Congress studying a departmental budget allotment: *use it or lose it*. There are two main reasons birds let go of their allotted flight: they did not need to escape predators in the air; they did not need to fly for food (and thus for migration). In several cases, the birds live (or lived) on remote islands that are free of predators—or *were* free, until man, in his island-hopping travels, introduced them. The flightless birds that belong to families in which the kin species fly—the rails, grebes, cormorants, and ducks—are all isolated on islands.

Some birds, such as the roadrunner, choose to walk—or run—even to a high perch.

Some of these birds, such as the dodo, had evolved into a rather minimalistic mode of life compared to the frenetic agitation we see in the skittish birds around us today. The dodo was not only flightless, it was slow afoot; and it was not only slow afoot, but free of fear. It allowed the Portuguese and Dutch mariners who found its islands to walk right up and wring its neck, literally and figuratively. The humans who found dodos failed the first test of conservation, and possibly the test of humaneness as well: they seem to have been unable to resist killing every fat, funny dodo they came across. The few who might have gotten wary were finished off by nest-robbing monkeys and pigs the sailors left behind on the islands. This happened very quickly, giving the dodo no time to regain the keeled sternum, flight muscles, trimness, or breadth of wing it had taken centuries to lose through natural atrophy.

The great auk—another recent extinction that human hunters have on their hands—did not need to fly around the endless ice of its Arctic habitat. There was no food on land, there were no predators the bird could not better escape in the ocean—where, incidentally, there *was* food—so the wings became flippers and the bird became aquatic. It waddled ashore only to breed. The great auk even migrated by sea, swimming as far south as Massachusetts for the relatively mild winters there.

The food and physical environment of many flightless birds—or preferentially flightless ones—has encouraged them to forage and escape afoot. Rails live in dense reeds, feeding on aquatic invertebrates and are so secretive that some scientists speculate there are species yet to be discovered. The first nest of the yellow rail was not found in North America until 1915, though the bird had been sighted much earlier and its nest had been sought in marshes for more than a century. All rails dislike flying, preferring to scramble through the reeds unseen. They don't need to fly to get food —it is captured in shallow water. So why take off?

The same can be said for the flightless cormorants and steamer ducks. Like the auk, they can get what they need by swimming; like the flightless rail species, they live on islands free of predators. The kiwi—the world's only truly *wingless* bird—does not enjoy freedom from things that would like to eat it, but it has evolved a kind of benign invisibleness that lets it go about its business of rooting for worms without calling attention to itself. The main strategy it has adopted is nocturnal life: it sleeps in its burrows during the day and noses around quietly at night.

The huge birds we call ratites (which means raft, from the description of them as "flat-bottomed boats" in contrast to the birds that have "keels" on the breastbone for the attachment of flight muscles) are surrounded by predators, too, but they have chosen to face them in broad daylight, and accordingly they have evolved aggressive skills. These birds have spectacular vision (elevated to observatory heights on long necks), pugnacious attitudes (enhanced by their size, especially when the wings are spread threateningly), and the legs of sprinters (which can also be used for bone-crunching kicks). Ostriches can outrun lions, and cassowaries can disembowel them with a long spike on the inside toe of each foot. These birds roam the plains, feeding on invertebrates that live on the ground. They weigh a lot. They can fight. What price flying? A price, evidently, that is far too high to be worth the energy.

There are four kinds of flight, with special wing adaptations for each. Obviously, all birds flap a bit, especially at takeoff, and all birds glide a little, too; but a bird's flight type is the one that dominates its wing work when it is aloft.

- *Flapping* is the busiest and the most common: the bird propels itself wing beat by wing beat. Passerines and most waterfowl depend heavily on flapping.
- *Soaring,* or passive gliding, is the least busy: the bird finds updrafts caused by hot air rising ("thermals") or by prevailing winds lifting over such obstructions as mountain ridges, and rides them upward on wings held straight out like sails. Large hawks, eagles, and condors are the best soarers.
- *Dynamic soaring* is a strange balance of falling and climbing in which a bird at sea (where there are no thermals) dives *with* the wind, then turns and banks upward *into* the wind, using the momentum of its coasting fall to drive it into a tough lift in the teeth of the air current. Then it dives again. Dynamic gliders rarely flap, but they work harder than any other type of flier to keep themselves constantly ahead of gravity. Albatrosses are the champions of this feat; they also stay in the air more than other birds, which isn't surprising—dynamic soaring is flight manufactured entirely from flight.

- *Hovering,* in which the wings beat or the feathers flutter in such a way that the bird hangs in one place in the air is the fourth type of flight. Kestrels and kingfishers hover occasionally, but the hummingbirds are the only ones that make a living at it.

The ruffed grouse can fly a quick dash to get away from trouble, but it would prefer to walk.

To hover, hummingbirds loop their wings backward and forward in a figure-8 motion. They are the only birds that can rotate their shoulders this way; other hoverers, such as kestrels and kingfishers, do so by riffling extended wings into the wind.

In general, flappers have shorter wings, more pointed at the tip; soarers have long, broad wings with rounded (sometimes almost squared) tips; dynamic soarers have extremely long, thin wings, with pointed tips. But within these broad outlines, individual species exhibit many variations, as they do in the style of flight. For example, goldfinches are flappers, but after a spell of furious flapping they stop, cruise downward, and hover for a moment before pulling themselves back up with more wing beats; most woodpeckers fly this way, too.

Flapping is the least understood type of flight, probably because it is the only type completely produced from within the bird. An understanding of the physics of air temperature and topography, or climb gradients versus wind speed, don't explain how a flapping wing flies. Neither, really, does a technical comprehension of the mechanics of flapping flight. We know that primaries function as propellers, how body weight is balanced, how lift is achieved, how the bones move, how the tendons are channeled, and how the air streams by. But we can't put it all together.

Fortunately, the bird, unburdened by self-conscious incomprehension, can put it all together with a flick of its wings.

Hunting Without Hands, Eating Without Teeth

Horror mongers from Hieronymus Bosch to Alfred Hitchcock have long played on one of our most secret, intuitive fears: we are scared of beaks. Put a couple of projecting horny mandibles on an otherwise harmless being's face and we recoil with a shudder, probably raising a hand to protect our eyes. Even when we expect a creature to have a beak, it's no comfort to our instincts. Let a tiny, common bird—a wren, say—fly straight at a big strong human, and what does Homo sapiens think about as he flails and covers up? Certainly not the whip of the whirring wings, the scrabbling grasp of the twiggy feet, the blunt impact of the 2-ounce body. No, what the human fears is the 1/2-inch spike of keratin under the beady little eyes.

Our fear of beaks is pretty legitimate, actually (though it would be more so if we were the size of shrews). As children we stare in horror at mouths, which seem the focal point of danger in roaring lions, grinning killer whales, barking dogs. Our terror of nasty tools and weapons from the man-made world is more sophisticated and abstract, but just as elemental.

Well, the beak is all of these things: a mouth, a tool, and a weapon in one piece, capable of all kinds of spearing, slashing, crunching, and gulping. It is far more potent than most objects in our worst dreams. To carry out the variety of nifty violence an owl can wreak with its bill, the lion would have to wield a bowie knife and a huge pair of forceps to augment its already capable jaws—and even then, the lack of a single omnipotent projection would make the effect less severe.

Aside from the threatening protrusion of the bird beak, there is something else: the hard thing sticking out from the face is simply *strange*. The strangeness only increases when we look at how many different kinds of bills there are. All birds have them; but no other gross ornithological feature varies as much in size and shape. The function is even a mystery sometimes—what in the world can a toucan *do* with that thing, or a parrot, or a crossbill?

Eat, first of all. The spikes, spears, hooks, sieves, wedges, tweezers, brushes, juicers, filters, chisels, nutcrackers, cleavers, scoops, spoons, suction pipettes, awls, knives, insect nets, jackhammers, pincers, and shears make a lot more sense when we look at fish darting through water, beetles hiding under bark, gnats flitting through the twi-

Facing page: African spoonbill.

The bill, unlike feathers, is supplied with blood that keeps it alive and growing; note the arteries inside the lower mandible of this hornbill.

Among fishing birds, kingfishers are much smaller than pelicans and ospreys; they lack the whip necks of anhingas and herons; they cannot swim as deftly as mergansers and cormorants. As compensation, most species have been blessed with a huge set of pincers for snatching fish deftly from the water.

light, grubs grubbing through the loam, drops of nectar nestling at the bottom of flowers, nut meats secure inside stony shells, seeds stuck in cones and catkins, plankton awash in oceans, oysters inside shells, mutton inside sheepskins. Almost everything growing in the wild is food to one kind of bird or another, and the bill is what the bird relies on not only to chew it, but first to capture and in many cases to kill it.

We could say that the bill is an honorary member of the digestive tract because it is usually the most visible indicator of a specialization that goes from esophagus to anus. With a little training, we can often tell what a bird eats by glancing at its bill, and usually we can infer something about its salivary glands, gizzard, and intestines, too. While we may be able to deduce a diet from the look of a bill, doing the reverse—sketching a bill from the look of a food item—is much more difficult.

Insect eaters include the pileated woodpecker, avocet, nightjar, bee eater, and kestrel, yet their beaks differ radically. This is because the insects must be sought in different places, through different actions. To find its bugs, the pileated woodpecker chisels 3- to 6-inch hunks of wood out of trees, excavating huge holes it then pries into; for this it needs a long, thick bill that can cut hardwood like an ax and yet be manipulated deftly. The avocet uses its delicate, upturned (recurved) bill to pluck insects and other invertebrates from shallow water, swishing its head from side to side as it wades; the thin beak slices through the water without much resistance. Nightjar bills are basically flying holes: these birds catch their insects by whipping through the air with their mouths gaping. The beak is a mere formality—a pair of horn lips that have little to do with ingestion. The bee eater has a fine pair of tweezers with which to snatch and disarm its prey. It needs to be careful: unlike many other birds that eat hymenoptera, bee eaters are not immune to the venom in its stingers and sacs. So, after catching the prey in the tip of its long beak, the bird takes it to a perch to rub and bash it against a branch or stone until the venom (along with various fragile body parts and fluids) has been squeezed out of the body, which is then eaten relatively whole. The kestrel is a tiny falcon, and hunts like one, swooping to take a grasshopper in its talons much as a peregrine would take a songbird, and butchering the prey with its hooked beak.

Seed eaters have more bill features in common, because their food doesn't vary nearly as much as insects: a seed is a seed, and it doesn't move around much. Generally these birds have short, conical bills, much larger next to the jaw, where the most intense pressure can be applied to the tough hulls. Inside the beak of some, such as the hawfinch, are knobs and ridges that serve as mortar and pestle for cracking and grinding the nuts and seeds. The hawfinch can handle even the pits of cherries and olives.

To a lesser degree than the insect eaters, the seed eaters show that bills are designed not only for consuming food, but also for seizing it. Goldfinches and siskins, which extract thin seeds from bristly thistles, have thinner bills than grosbeaks, which reach their preferred buds and fruit pits very easily. The most extravagant adaptation of a beak to the task of eating seeds is that of the crossbill, whose upper mandible curves one way while the lower curves the other, so that the assembly looks rather like a pair of scissors someone stepped on. The beak is designed to slip the seeds from the interior narrows of evergreen cones, and it works better than it might appear.

Raptors' bills resemble each other, from the saw-whet owl to the monkey-eating eagle. Though they are strong, these killing beaks are not especially long or stout. They gain their deadly power from one feature of structural design: the upper mandible, longer than the bottom, is turned down in a fierce hook. When the raptor closes its beak on a vole or rabbit, this hook quickly dispatches the unfortunate prey: stabs it, holds it securely, gives extra leverage for a bite or twist to the backbone, and, once the prey is dead, tears its meat into edible shreds. Owls swallow their prey whole, but most raptors butcher; the

The crow, a virtual omnivore, has an all-purpose beak good for everything from crunching potato chips in a park to killing mice in a field.

Wading and tweezing. (avocet)

The red crossbill scissors seeds from cones and catkins.

The red-tailed hawk shows its classic raptor's beak.

The lappet-faced vulture's entire head is streamlined so it can be stuck deep into the messy cavities of carrion and withdrawn relatively clean.

The bills of toucans are huge but light, allowing them to grasp fruits dangling out of most birds' reach in the jungle canopy. The bills are good at carving the fruit, too, with notches along the mandibular edge for extra bite.

prey is often too large to gulp in one bite, and their digestive systems are not as well-equipped as the owl's to separate the inedible parts from the meat.

Fruit eaters have hooks, and in terms of forces applied, they function like the raptors' beaks. But the skin they pierce is that of mango or papaya, and their crunching is reserved for nuts and seeds. The hook is hammer to the anvil of a strong, notched lower mandible in birds such as the cockatoo, providing a beak that can crack the hardest fruit pits. Some fruit eaters have huge bills—the toucans and hornbills look almost like cartoons. The exaggerated length of their beaks serves mainly to extend their reach for fruit on vines in the forest canopy they inhabit; the ferocious bite implied by the swordlike mandibles is not really used.

Fish eaters' bills perhaps most dramatically emphasize the need to catch prey over the need to chew it. Very few fisherbirds butcher their meat; most swallow it whole. Therefore, no bill features are spent on mastication, so important to the seed eaters. Instead, the bills of fish eaters show as broad a variety of shapes and sizes as those of the insectivorous birds, because fish, like insects, hide in all sorts of places, and move in all sorts of ways.

The anhinga is a perfect example of a bird whose beak is for catching only. This feathered

The nut-cracking beak is a hard-used tool, more like a hammer-and-anvil than a mouth. (palm cockatoo)

submarine, which cruises through warm waterways with only its neck sticking above the surface like an S-shaped periscope, almost looks as if it has no head or bill—its neck just seems to taper off to a point, with an eye set a few inches back from the end. Of course, the anhinga does have a skull and beak, but these bony parts flow without protrusion from the sleek line of the neck, making the head a perfect aquadynamic spear. The anhinga puts it to the use implied by its shape, and sticks it straight through a fish, broadside. Somehow, by shaking its head, the bird loosens the fish from its gig, and swallows it whole, headfirst.

There aren't many other birds who impale fish this way—even the similar blades of herons, bitterns, and egrets are usually used as pincers. The streamlined spear shape lets these birds move their heads through water without losing much velocity or angle of attack. The beak must be opened at the last millisecond and snapped on the fish at the end of a fierce thrust from above the water, with an intuitive calculation for the visual refraction.

Pelicans use what may be the simplest fishing technique. This large diving bird chases fish seen from the sky and scoops them into an expandable pouch slung from the lower mandible. The pouch makes the bill into a flexible fish trap, with the top mandible as the lid. Pelicans don't swallow the water they trap along with the fish; they must leak it out, rather slowly, until only the fish remain to be gulped.

Skimmers have special lower mandibles, too: flattened and elongated into a blade that protrudes far beyond the tip of the upper. This awkward-looking beak permits the skimmer to capture and eat prey without missing a wing beat—a rare skill among sea birds. The skimmer flies low, with its beak open and lower mandible

Wielding a mean spear: anhinga with bluegill.

When a snowy egret snaps its neck like this, chances are it will come up with a fish.

A beak precisely adapted to the method of food gathering: the black skimmer,
who slices through the water with its longer lower mandible, hoping to strike a fish
it can then pinch with the upper one.

cutting through the water. When the long blade touches something, the head snaps downward and the upper mandible closes on the crustacean or fish, which is then dragged above the surface and swallowed. The key sense is touch, through the lower part of the bill. This means the skimmer needn't depend on high scouting flight, as many of the other fishers do, or even on daylight; skimmers often feed at night.

Many birds that pursue fish underwater have slightly hooked upper mandibles—cormorants, gannets, boobies, albatrosses, shearwaters. They are using the better part of their bodies to swim, and thus depend on their bills to make the quick, sure snatch of slippery prey. Loons, however, have straight, strong beaks, as do most penguins and kingfishers.

The beaks of the merganser family show a fishing adaptation that seems so good one would expect it to be more widespread. These diving ducks have long, thin bills with serrated margins and hooks on the tip. The sawtooth design looks like just the thing to grip a squirming smelt. Perhaps mergansers need the extra grip because their jaws are less powerful than other fishers, who do well enough with straight-edged snapping.

Most other ducks do not really fish—they eat invertebrates nibbled out of the mud on pond bottoms, along with morsels of plant life. Their beaks are flat and broad, perfect for munching water-lily roots or spooning through mud for insect larvae and crustaceans.

A last classification of beak types could be called "the generalist": the straight, usually pointed bill that serves birds whose diet includes a variety of foods. Omnivores and scavengers such as gulls, ravens, and crows need to be able to do everything from opening a cracked mussel to gutting a road-kill skunk. Their beaks are adaptable to the matter at hand—tools that may not be as good at specific tasks as those of the crossbill or snail kite or sapsucker, but which are better overall for the improvisatory demands a piece of odd food might make.

The chapter on flight pointed out the bill's features of strength and lightness, especially compared to mammalian teeth, and emphasized the contribution of this unique mouth design to the general aerodynamic trim of the skull.

Perhaps the most important aspect of beak-skull mechanics, however, is *cranial kinesis*. This "skull motion" simply means that birds can move both of their jaws, upper and lower, relative to the braincase. The jaws, of course, are connected to the mandibular bones, which are sheathed in horn, to become the bill.

Obviously, the bird's ability to use the two-piece tool it has been given in the form of a bill increases if it can command both pieces. We ought to know: like all mammals, we can move only our lower jaw and this reduces the usefulness of our mouths for any kind of grasping. For one thing, using the mouth this way means changing the position of the whole head, throwing off the spatial orientation—which would be very distracting if we had to eat and watch for predators at the same time. Notice how we tilt our head backward to get a good bite at an apple. Foxes and long-snouted dogs seem to have it better, but not by much; they have to move their heads entirely, too.

It is also much easier to catch something—a fish, a grasshopper, even a cherry hanging from a stem—between two pincers moving in coordination than to catch it between a moving pincer and a stationary one. This can be demonstrated in a simple experiment. Hold your arms out in front of you stiffly and have someone throw a Frisbee at you. Try to catch it by raising your top arm and lowering your bottom one, bringing the hands together onto the spinning disk. Then try again with your top arm held out straight. Without raising or lowering it, catch the Frisbee

Galapagos mockingbirds use their long, sharp beaks to pierce an albatross's egg and suck it dry.

Form Follows Food

In the chapter on flight we demonstrated the designer's adage, "Form follows function," noting how the bird's physiology and structure evolved around the function of flight. We could perhaps say the same thing for feeding. Some flight scientists might argue that the formal evolutions that have followed the function of eating are limited mainly to the beak; but an internist might reply that in many species flight itself is merely a servant of digestion—simply a means for finding and delivering food to the gastrointestinal tract.

There are quite a few birds in whom the dietary habits do seem to be the *primum mobile,* to say the least. The major internal or external features of such birds (often quite peculiar features) can perhaps be understood only through an understanding of what it eats.

The flamingo is a stimulating case for such nutritional ratiocination. Here we have a bird who looks like what would happen if two strong kids fought over a duck in tug-of-war fashion: one took the feet, the other grabbed the head, and they pulled frantically in opposite directions. A compact body is perched on the longest legs this side of the ostrich; squiggling out from the body like a spent streamer is an equally long neck, ending in a big beak with a sharp crook in it.

Flamingos feed on organic matter in the mud at the bottom of the water they wade in. They are equipped to digest everything from bacteria to algae to insect larvae to fish—a huge dietary range in terms of the food's size and biochemical makeup, but a very narrow one in terms of its ecology. To get food of such a variety of shapes and sizes, the flamingo lowers its head into the water, lays its open beak's *upper* surface on the bottom, and swishes its upside-down head back and forth in a sweep through the ooze. The mud is taken into the troughlike beak with water; the mandibles—specially equipped with stiff lamellae comparable to the baleen of some whales—are brought close together so that the lamellae form a strainer along the entire opening. The huge tongue pushes the watery muck through this strainer. What stays in the mouth is food.

The awkward hoatzin.

Like a baleen whale that gulps tons of plankton-bearing water, the flamingo must take in a great amount of the medium in which its food lives—the ratio of food content to mud volume is tiny. The long neck lets the bird sweep its collecting tool through long stretches of mud in a single motion, which greatly increases the scope of the beak. The long-stepping legs, of course, increase the scope of the neck that increase the scope of the beak, and so on; neck and legs and beak go together to make a very efficient feeder.

The everglade kite, which feeds only on a single species of freshwater snail in a very limited marsh environment in Florida, has the world's most specialized beak. Its upper mandible is an exaggerated hook—extreme even when compared to the beaks of hawks—allowing it to follow the curve of the shell of its prey and get a grip on the animal deep inside the spiraling recesses. But the beak of the hoatzin is very specialized, too, and though the adaptation looks less dramatic than the kite's, it anticipates greater internal and behavioral changes as consequences of food.

The hoatzin is the only bird in the world whose diet consists mostly of leaves. Its beak is rather like a short scissors, with sharp mandibular blades that cut leaves into strips that the bird then swallows. The next step into the digestive tract, however, shows how the bird's diet has transformed it into a curiosity.

The hoatzin has a crop 50 times larger than its stomach and tougher than its gizzard. Most of its food-breakdown takes place right here in the foremost chamber of its digestive system, grinding the extremely fibrous leaves to paste with strong muscles and horny surfaces. The crop's volume completely alters the bird's physique: it is top-heavy, which makes it awkward at flying, standing, or even perching; in fact, the hoatzin generally sort of just *leans*, propping its crop-swelled upper breast against branches. The sternum has a special outer covering—a kind of callus—just for this purpose.

This bird does not like to fly. It prefers to *climb*, using its wings like arms for balance and pulling itself through the vegetation, breaking its flight feathers, wobbling as its burdened thorax heaves this way and that. When it does take to the air its flight looks more like a guided leap from one thick tree to the next; the flight feathers are poorly developed and the tail must be flapped. Its feet are not particularly good at taking grip, either, so it sometimes leaves its wings out to catch itself in a sprawl among the leaves.

Young hoatzins are better equipped than adults for arboreal ascent: they are born with gripping claws on the front of their wings, a unique development of digits that are usually internal and vestigial in other birds. The claws help them scramble while grazing in the branches, from which they nevertheless often fall into the waters below their habitual nesting places. The chicks are also naturally born good swimmers; after some weeks, though, they lose their hands *and* their swimming ability, leaving them literally up a tree.

The wing-claws and, in fact, the whole appearance of the hoatzin calls to mind the first bird, Archeopteryx, which was also a branch leaper and climber. Some ornithologists have suggested that the hoatzin is a freakish relic, a horseshoe crab or coelacanth of the bird kingdom. Whether this judgment is true or not, it is a bird whose primary job seems to be surviving the awkwardness imposed on it by its choice of food—something that could be said of any bird.

by moving only the lower hand up against the top one. Imagine fishing for a two-inch minnow like this. Obviously, the bill of a bird can open wider and then close on something with greater dexterity, speed, and force if both its parts move together.

The skeletal and muscular arrangement that allows cranial kinesis makes for complicated mandibular joints. This may sound as if birds are more fragile, but the opposite is true—another important advantage for them. A complicated joint, in this case, is a joint insulated against shock: when a bird strikes something with its beak, the

A northern flicker sends the chips flying.

jolt is absorbed by many parts—bones, muscles, and tendons break the singular impact down into bearable increments, as it were. With our extremely simple jaw, an impact on the chin goes directly to the joint and on to the braincase, *bam-bam*; we would make lousy woodpeckers. But birds can hammer away without jarring the brain, rattling the eyes in their sockets, or fracturing the tiny bones of the ears. They can even afford to have lighter skulls, which, as we know, is important for getting off the ground.

Being able to move the parts of the bill—even though the top mandible cannot move all that much—makes the bill a more sensitive part of the organism. In fact, the beak may be the *most* sensitive part of the bird.

Although this certainly doesn't look as if it could be true, the bill is tough to the touch, and very hard-used. Imagine cracking hickory nuts with a sensitive organ! The beak's horny covering is created by the same kind of Malpighian cells that make feathers, and feathers are dead; they "feel" only because the follicles in which they sit are sconces of nerve cells. Wouldn't beaks be the same?

No. Beaks are not dull plates of solid keratin *near* nerves. They are fully alive, loaded with generative cells and receptors for tactile stimulation, comparable in sensitivity to our lips and fingertips. Indeed, a duck bill is supplied with certain touch-sensitive nerve endings to a far greater degree than one of our fingers.

Thus, the snipe that sticks its beak into the ground is not just playing a game of blind luck, hoping it will spear a worm by utter chance; it is very sensitively *probing*. The bill not only recognizes the touch of a worm, but also feels disturbances in the soil from a worm boring nearby—and then goes and gets it. Woodcocks, with especially pliable bills and mobile upper mandibles, can thrust their beaks into the ground, detect a worm close by, and snag it without moving their heads. A hairy woodpecker will rap out a shallow hole, then place the tip of its beak into it, lightly. If the bird feels vibrations of bugs

Some hornbill beaks are worn like crowns; others are worked hard as weapons.

moving beneath this minimal penetration, it excavates deeper. If not, it moves a few inches and tries again with another groove.

Many birds feed by feel. The sandpipers and other shorebirds, the waders, the dabbling ducks, flamingos, woodpeckers, wood storks, skimmers, swallows, and swifts cutting through the dark— all depend on the flicker of touch in searching for prey. And it is very efficient to have the organ of touch also be the organ of seizure and ingestion. Imagine the woodpecker pulling its beak out of a hole and having to reach in with its foot to get a bug.

Another benefit of a living bill is that it can grow—specifically, it can generate tissue to replace parts that have worn away. The tip of the beak is the bird's main point of active contact with the world. It is so well-used that cells naturally wear away and the bill would eventually become blunt and less sensitive if new cells were not at the ready. In some cases of chickens and storks, beaks and mandibular bones have been known to regenerate even after severe damage.

This kind of growth is different from molting, in which an entire worn feather is jettisoned seasonally and a new one pops out to take its place. This is a natural process of cell replace-ment for repair and maintenance, more like the process that keeps us from wearing away our fingertips or the soles of our feet. There are partial bill molts in certain species, but the parts that are cast off are special appendages grown for the breeding season. Atlantic puffins, for example, spruce up for courtship with curvaceous, brilliantly striped sheaths covering their straight, black bills. After summer, when the party is over and the offspring have reached adolescence, the sheath falls off in nine neat pieces.

Many other species show color changes in the beak without any such change in shape. Starlings have a black beak that turns hot yellow as breeding time arrives; the bills *and* feet of Arctic terns go from black to reddish orange in the spring, and back to black in the fall. These chromatic primpings are caused by hormonal activity. Perhaps fittingly, beak-brightening occurs mainly in species that do not molt to flashy breeding plumage, but stick with the same feather coloration year-round.

There is more to a beak than simply a couple of mandibles, though the gross outer structure is its most definitive feature. The beak is also the housing for the nostrils and the tongue. In most

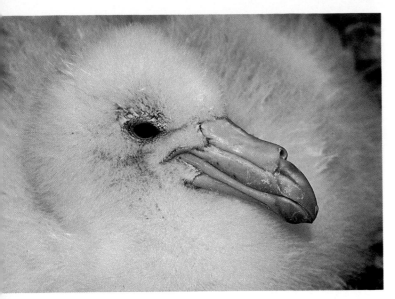

The tubenoses, all seabirds, have external nostrils for expelling salt in high concentrations. (southern giant petrel)

birds, nostrils serve the same two purposes as those of mammals: they take in air as an alternative to mouth-breathing and they contain or lead to the outermost receptors for smell. Birds do not have keen olfactory abilities, as a rule.

The kiwi, which tromps around at night digging for earthworms, has been blessed with the bird kingdom's greatest nose, perhaps in compensation for its lack of the wings and keen vision common to other birds. The kiwi's extraordinary sense of smell has an extraordinary physiognomy, too: its nostrils are not found at the base of the upper bill, as in all other birds, but are located near the tip of the lower mandible. This makes quite a difference when your beak is 8 inches long and you keep it stuck in the earth most of the time—nostrils up near the myopic eyes wouldn't have much chance of detecting earthworms down there in the loam.

There are several distinct kinds of nostrils, or external nares. Birds of prey have open nostrils set in a fleshy growth, the cere, at the base of the top mandible. Doves and pigeons have nostrils *covered* by a fleshy growth, the operculum, which blocks all but a slit of the airway. The nares of grouse, crows, and ravens are covered with small, flat feathers; those of frogmouths and nightjars

are surrounded by bristles. Shearwaters, petrels, and albatrosses have such a distinctive nostril configuration that they are classified as tubenoses for the reedlike structures set along their top mandibles, leading to the nares.

In all of these birds and most others, the perforations are open, whatever their covering; they lead to the nasal passages, glands, and olfactory receptors. However, in several of the adult diving birds—cormorants, anhingas, frigate birds, and gannets—the nares are closed. Some of these birds are forced to breathe through open beaks. The gannets and cormorants have an alternative, though; they have evolved a tiny permanent gape at the juncture of upper and lower mandibles, that allows them to inhale and exhale with their mouths closed. The opening is covered by a movable lid when they dive underwater (gannets plummet headfirst from on high and hit the water with great impact).

Nostrils have a unique importance to most seabirds because they lead to nasal glands that help to clear the body of the excess salt consumed when the bird drinks seawater. The ocean has a saline concentration of about 3.5 percent. The birds who live on it drink regularly, even eschewing freshwater that may be nearby. But like any non-aquatic animal, birds must keep the concentration of salt in body fluids to about 1 percent. There is no conditioning of the circulatory and renal systems to accept more—too much salt means dehydration and death, as much for an albatross that spends its whole life at sea as an Iowa farmer who never gets within 500 miles of it. Avian kidneys, less effective even than man's at leaching out the salt, cannot handle the triple load seawater contains, so seabirds such as murres, albatrosses, geese, terns, and gulls have well-developed glands in their nasal cavities, to which the circulatory system delivers the excess salt in the blood. The glands extract it and then secrete a highly concentrated saline fluid the birds spew out as waste. The salt glands, as they are called, can be as much as ten times more efficient than our kidneys at removing salt.

Like the nostrils, the birds' tongue is a sensory

The kiwi sticks its bill deep into the ground to probe for worms. With nostrils at its tip, this bill is the best organ of smell in the bird world.

organ and in many species a vital conduit for food. Tongues vary in their size, shape, and function as much as the bills that house them, largely for the same reason: the foods birds pursue vary wildly in form, material, and location. Tongues, too, are honorary members of the digestive system—they are adapted to be complementary to their beaks—and the interior organs depend on these outer parts functioning effectively. There are tongues that serve the primary purpose of collecting food, tongues that help in the first breakdown of it, and tongues that simply guard the entrance of the mouth.

The most aggressive collecting tongues belong to the woodpeckers. Once our pileated woodpecker has chopped out its hole, the bill's work is done; there will be no seek-and-squeeze pinching of beetle larvae between the mandibles. The bugs exposed by the beak's chops are gathered in by the incredibly long, barb-tipped tongue. Coated with sticky saliva, this nearly prehensile dart shoots in among the bugs and pulls them easily into the mouth.

Most woodpeckers can stick their tongues out more than twice the length of their beaks. The green woodpecker extends its tongue four times its bill's length. The extension, however, is not *all* tongue: most of it is the two snaky cartilaginous hyoid bones, into which the tongue is set. The hyoid structures in a woodpecker are folded up accordion-like in their unextended form. They begin at the base of the beak's interior, not far from where the tongue is rooted, and proceed toward the back of the head, curving down beneath the skull, up over the cranium, down through an eye socket, and forward over the point where they started, at last to the root of the tongue. The woodpecker can call upon this well-rooted length when it wants to search a deep crack for ants, extending it as needed.

Sapsuckers and hummingbirds also have tongues that collect their food. The sapsucker's is tipped with a hairy burr that absorbs sap by capillary attraction, while the hummingbird's, extensible and usually forked at the end, is rolled

The beaks of the sunbirds are made for finding the secrets of flowers.

into a tube that drains the nectar from flowers. An old theory that the hummingbird sucked through its tongue like a straw does not, alas, hold nectar; the tongue simply makes a very efficient channel. The hummingbird shoots it back and forth into the flower very rapidly, and swallows the flow of nectar conducted to its palate.

Many seed eaters have active tongues that deftly manipulate their food in the process of cracking nuts; parrots are especially adroit this way. Finches break hulls with their beaks and extract kernels with their tongues, using them a moment later —after the kernel is swallowed—to flick away the empty husk. The tongues of most seed and insect eaters are not extravagantly formed; they fit well within the contours of the lower mandible and assist in the initial processing and subsequent swallowing of food.

Most birds that swallow prey whole have *un-der*developed tongues—too much of a protrusion gets in the way when you're trying to gulp a stickleback or a mole. But some fish eaters, such as penguins and mergansers, have good-sized tongues that help with the gulping, due to one-way projections pointing backward toward the esophagus. These sticky spines rise if a fish tries to slither back out the way it came.

Bills do a good job of putting food inside the body. Like any tool or weapon, however, bills operate only when they have been placed in the right position. A woodpecker flapping in the air around the trunk of a tree isn't going to put that marvelous chisel to work unless it finds a way to situate itself on the bark. A cormorant won't hook a fish it cannot catch up with underwater. Some birds feed and hunt while in flight or from perches. But for most others, wings can do no more than deliver them to the area in which the food must be found and eaten. The rest is up to their legs and feet.

As noted in the flight chapter, birds are generally not made for walking. Their center of gravity is set to maintain a good balance in flight; often this means that the legs are lower or farther back in the body than they would be in an ambulatory creature. The problem is compounded in the floating swimmers, who depend on webbed feet to propel them in the water from behind—their legs are so far back that some, such as loons, can barely walk at all.

But criticizing the design of a bird because it doesn't walk well is like complaining that a violin makes a terrible baseball bat. Birds don't need to walk well. They hop or hobble just enough to get by. However, it would be a mistake to assume their lower limbs were mere formalities—birds do need to grasp perches of all kinds, squeeze and carry prey, scratch in the dirt for food, and wade, swim, and defend themselves—they even do such extremely specialized things as treading on floating lily pads or deep, soft snow. For all of these they need hind limbs capable of actions that complement the beak's specific powers.

What we think of as the foot of a bird is really just its toes, usually four of them, three pointing forward and one to the rear. What we think of as the leg—the little scaly stick that juts up from the "foot" into the feathers—is the tarsus, cor-

The ostrich runs the plains on heavy, flat-bottomed, two-toed feet.

With these, the merlin plucks birds right out of the air.

responding to the main part of a human foot between heel and toe. The first joint that looks like a knee bending the wrong way is not the knee, but the heel (bending the right way after all). Beneath the feathers lie the bird's true knee and thigh.

The upper leg renders a service to the foot, without which the bird would never be able to relax on a perch. Tendons called flexors run from the knee down the back of the tarsus to the toes. When the bird grips a perch and relaxes, it goes into a kind of crouch, bending its knees; this tightens the flexors all the way to the end of the line—which means the toes automatically clench. The grip on the perch tightens involuntarily, so the bird does not have to stand there consciously squeezing. It can sleep securely.

The work of the foot is often just as subtle. A flicker jacking up and down a vertical trunk is taking a keen grip with each shift of position, and its feet are making a series of spontaneous adjustments to changes in the irregular surface of the bark. The individual toes splay out as needed, or pull in; the claws on the end curl into crevices, or spread over smooth spots. The body angle that presses the feet *into* their grip —as opposed to pressing with gravity away from the grip—is instinctively calculated and maintained. The flicker doesn't stop and plan each toehold, of course, any more than we scrutinize the possibilities for our fingers when we pick up a soapy plate in dishwater.

Feet can take far more aggressive roles in the quest for food. Raptors strike prey first with their

The oxpecker would rather preen a warthog's body than its own: the warthog features ticks to eat.

The rear limb can be as powerful in grappling and reaching as a human arm. Seen here: a martial eagle clutching a ground squirrel and a red-tailed hawk fighting a diamondback rattlesnake.

feet, often killing it with the impact of the hit. The sharp, protruberant talons of the raptor make other birds' claws look like toenails, and the grip is viciously powerful. Often, for an owl or hawk, a quick squeeze breaks the spine of a freshly nabbed mammal or reptile. If a bite is necessary, the feet keep the prey under control until the coup de grace is administered.

A raptor's kill can be very large. Golden eagles have been known to take sheep, and a harrier —rather a spindly bird of prey—will leap at the chance to slash a rabbit ten times its weight. Taking a big corpse back to the nest is a challenge most raptors do not back away from— they will dig in the claws and flap until they drag it off the ground or exhaust themselves trying. For these arduous transports, the bird counts on the indefatigable grip of the claws, and they seldom fail.

Sometimes their grasp is too resolute. A naturalist watched an osprey drowned by a lungfish it had grabbed by the back; the fish was too large

for the bird to pull from the water, but its talons were too deep to let go. When the fish dove, the bird went with it. Another observer watched an eagle hauling a stoat it had snatched from the ground. The bird stubbornly held on and kept flying as the stoat twisted this way and that, until it was able, in midair, to bite its way up the bird's leg, ultimately to the breast.

Most birds' feet don't let them in for this kind of trouble. Waders—the best walkers among flying birds—do nothing more than take steps with theirs, balancing well on slippery pond bottoms or rocky shores with their long toes. The jacana takes long toes (and nails) to an extreme; it looks like a plump bird wearing a photographer's tripods as shoes. These spindles displace its weight so delicately that it can walk on lily pads and rafts of vegetable matter.

The feet of gulls, terns, ducks, loons, geese, cormorants, gannets, albatrosses, boobies, and pelicans have evolved in the other direction. When these seabirds spread their toes, they create a

Pellets

Because birds have no teeth they swallow a lot of indigestible matter: insect chitin, shells of mollusks or crustaceans, seeds inside fruits, fur, feathers, bones, teeth, snakeskin, earth in various gritty forms, accidental objects. Some of this stuff is ground up in the gizzard, passed through the digestive tract, and defecated. Much of it, however, is collected by the muscular rolling of the gizzard into little oblong packages and regurgitated. The packages are called pellets, and when birds eject them orally, the action is rather prettily described as *casting the pellet*. (The term probably comes from the handsome language of falconry, the sport of kings.)

Birds of prey, which often eat entire vertebrates but are poor at digesting bone, produce pellets from every meal, usually 6 to 12 hours after eating. Experiments with captive raptors have shown that the birds must cast the pellet from the previous meal before eating the next—which is hardly surprising, considering the bulk of the pellet and the fact that it cannot be pushed farther down the digestive tract by incoming food. Pellets from birds of prey look like a child's attempt to put back together a creature that has been taken apart: the bones are lined up neatly and wrapped in a snug covering of fur, the whole oblong often resembling in shape (and of course, color) the animal it used to be—mouse, vole, shrew.

Hawks and eagles butcher their prey, so they may leave some indigestible bits on the carcass. But owls swallow animals whole. Thus an owl's pellets contain a full record of its diet and are prized for their completeness by scientists studying the food chain or, say, the geographical movements of small mammal populations. Owls such as the barn owl allow pellets to accumulate beneath the roost, and a pile may go back for years. The pellets can be roughly dated, and an analysis of their contents can reveal when a particular prey species was present in the area and when it moved on.

Ornithologists can also keep track of birds that have been preyed upon not just from feathers and bones, but also from aluminum leg bands that were attached to them for this purpose. Bands found in pellets sometimes reveal anomalies in migratory patterns that alert scientists to new movements or transient populations.

broad paddle instead of a spidery foot. Gulls, geese, and ducks swim a great deal afloat, paddling regularly with their feet below the waterline. Diving ducks, loons, and cormorants swim mostly underwater, stretching their necks and churning their feet with wings hugged to the sides. The others make quick vertical dives instead of swimming, but their webbed feet allow them to pursue a fish deeper than the dive takes them, or to navigate easily when afloat.

Land birds—pheasants, grouse, quail, turkeys, domestic fowl, finches, towhees, and sparrows—all scratch the earth or ground cover to turn up food. They have strong toes with well-developed nails, but the feet serve only as bush beaters: once something turns up, it is pecked with the bill. Not so with birds in the parrot family: they pick up a piece of food with one foot and bring it to the mouth much as we do. Parrots are even consistently right- or left-handed about it. Not to be outdone, the parrot's beak shows unusual versatility, too: when climbing through the tropical

This pellet contains the inedible parts of everything an owl swallowed in one day.

Birds of prey are not the only birds to make pellets: more than 325 species from 60 families have been found to eject undigested parts this way, and some researchers speculate that all insect eaters must form and cast pellets of accumulated chitin, just as all shorebirds who eat crustaceans do. This would raise the number of pelleteers considerably: somewhere between 80 to 90 percent of the world's birds eat insects.

The nature of the pellet depends not only on the bird's diet, but also on its digestion. Pellets of different species that eat much the same thing may be quite different because one species makes use of things that remain untouched, gastrically speaking, by the other. Heron pellets, for example, contain almost no bones—the green heron can digest more of the frog it catches than can the marsh hawk. Some birds cast pellets made up mostly of a single substance: wax from honey guides, chitin from swifts, fishbones from kingfishers. Omnivorous birds such as crows and gulls may produce wildly different pellets every day, depending on what they discover to plunder.

In addition to ejecting detritus, the formation and ejection of a pellet serves an additional purpose in birds, especially birds of prey: it scours the body passages that handle it—stimulating, cleaning, and generally conditioning the walls, especially of the gullet. Thus the regurgitation—although it requires a more convulsive effort from some birds than others—does not carry the same stigma of unpleasantness it does in humans. Even chicks form pellets. Some owlets begin casting them after only a week out of the shell.

canopy's dense growth of vines and trees, the bird will use the beak as a leading hand to pull itself up while the feet grasp below.

We keep discovering how birds live in the *world*, while maintaining—at least in our eyes —a strange kind of detachment from what we might call the *earth*. It is true that a life built around flight keeps them literally aloft, if not aloof. We don't see them burrowing into the side of a mountain, gorging in the midst of berry bushes, or swatting salmon out of a river, like a bear;

we don't see them stomping through muddy swamp and dense forest, rubbing flanks with twenty chums, like an elephant; we don't see them hugging trees, lollygagging, and eating bananas patiently, bite-by-hand–held-bite, like an orangutan. Mostly we see them sitting in trees or flying.

But perhaps flight has fooled us; we may be associating birds so much with the sky that we haven't noticed their integral earthiness. Waxwings gorge on berries, ospreys grab salmon, and swifts burrow into riverbanks. Herons stomp

Even the slickest fish can't squirm through this grip. The osprey not only has sharp talons that curve deeply; the inner surfaces of its toes bristle with spicules.

through swamps; toucans eat bananas—sometimes rather patiently. What's the difference?

As much as the strangeness of flight, it is the strangeness of beaks and claws and wings, instead of four similar limbs. Even if a wolf or elephant simply runs on its four legs, we feel akin to the way it addresses the ground. When an ape stands up, grabs a limb, hoists itself to a crook in a tree, and eats with its hand, we identify physically with every motion: She is in the same world I am. This doesn't happen when a roadrunner snatches a rattlesnake with its beak.

If we look at the equipment birds have been given, and see it not so much for its different form as for its similarity of function, we can feel ourselves drawing them into our sense of environment. They fly up there; but they also walk and fish and build and hunt and dig down here. For all of our sense of mammalian earthiness, we must admit that most creatures touch the planet primarily with their feet. What is different in the bird's stance? The feet are scaly and skinny

With long toes and delicate balance, walking on water—well, nearly—is no trick for the purple gallinule.

Webbed feet can walk on water, too, but only when it cannot be paddled through. (Canada geese)

with talons, but take a peek at the foot of a grizzly bear. We must also admit that most creatures delve into the environment primarily to eat; again, where is the avian distinction? We should not be fooled by the brittle horn that has replaced soft lips and white teeth—a mouth is a mouth, and an animal looking for something to put in it is involved in its surroundings, and ours.

Few birds with webbed feet can perch on limbs as confidently as this red-footed booby. Boobies' toes are long and the membranes between them are very thin and flexible.

The Artful Bird—
Singer and Builder

Humans really stretch out the personal processes of nature. We have long, lazy childhoods, urgent but basically irresponsible adolescences, finicky courtships, a rather effete sense of propagation, an offhand regard for home and work, and a ferocious devotion to extending old age. The whole string of events seems to be a matter of whimsy or rationale; we labor over a lot of choices and changes, and believe little is beyond our personal control.

Birds—which are pretty low in the hierarchy of intelligence, as humans estimate it, and therefore low in "initiative"—give a clear example of life governed directly by nature: there is a routine progression of urges that are fulfilled with no fooling around. When the hormones say jump, the bird jumps. Yet for all of this knee-jerking, the avian life is not without ceremony, creativity, or intricacy. How many of us in our first spring could build a filigree nest of pure saliva, like the Asian swift, or an indigo-festooned dance hall out of weeds and found objects, like the satin bowerbird?

The cycle of courtship and nesting shows the bird at its most hormone-enslaved, yet also re- veals its finest creative abilities. This is the time in which birds build their amazing architecture, sing their finest songs, nurture the fragile beauty of their eggs into the even more fragile homeliness of their chicks. It is the Renaissance of birddom, a blooming of arts and sciences.

Song

Anyone who has walked around during a solar eclipse has noticed a sudden eeriness in the atmosphere that has nothing to do directly with the superimposition of disks in the sky. Things are a little darker, as just before a rainstorm; but what *else* is it that makes the moment seem so different? We look around, we sniff, we try this sense and that, until at last we *listen*—and hear nothing. It is silent. The birds have stopped singing.

For many of us, only the subtraction of bird song can make us notice how much of it usually surrounds us. It is more or less always there, on the periphery of our awareness. We may not focus on it, but we *hear* it. We have probably

Facing page: Long-billed marsh wren.

made unconscious observations about it: when pressed, most of us would suppose that we hear it more during our jog in the early morning and our evening stint at the backyard grill than we do at midday; that it is more prevalent in summer than in winter. We could even guess that we hear several different songs from different birds, and that some of them are beautiful and others crude.

Bird song is something that sinks in despite our habitual indifference to it. Once we do become aware of it, we start to notice it everywhere; our ears, once tuned in, become acquisitive. But before this happens we mostly ignore what is probably the most universal contribution nature makes to the world of sound.

Why does song elude us? Even bird watchers come to a fascination with song late in their evolution of enthusiasms. Though birds are usually easier to hear than see, most birders use their binoculars exclusively in the beginning of their study. One reason may be that bird song seems so subtle, evanescent, and complicated. Standing in a forest and trying to distinguish the scarlet tanager's song from the red-eyed vireo's—was that a *tcheer tchee theerp* or a *tcheer tchup too-too*?—without a bird to *look* at, might seem as forbidding as analyzing the second oboe's harmonic pattern in a C. P. E. Bach sinfonia.

In fact, bird song *is* marvelously complicated. Each bird has several different songs serving different needs, and the songs are sung with infinite variations. Holding a thrush to a field guide's description of its song is like expecting Charlie Parker to play "Billie's Bounce" the same way twice.

Nevertheless, we can learn to recognize one bird's song—even in its variations—from another, just as we can distinguish Charlie Parker from Sonny Rollins, or Isaac Stern from Itzhak Perlman. First, we have to learn what the singing is all about.

Why Do Birds Sing?

Song is obviously so instinctive a behavior—and so haphazard in its frequency—that to infer an intent quest behind each chirp might seem absurdly anthropomorphic. Sometimes birds just sing for the sheer exuberance of it. But most of the time there seems to be a clear reason why a bird uses up the precious zest needed to produce song. We have seen before that a bird, with its frenzied metabolic needs and its demanding style of gathering food, wastes nothing that might preserve the slim margin of life between energy expended and energy consumed. Birds rarely fly for fun; they fly to find food, defend territory, or impress a mate. Birds don't do much that is trivial. They cannot afford the calories or the time.

Another indication of the importance of song is the apparatus developed to produce it. As we have noted, a bird's body is designed and assembled with nearly cruel economy; everything that can be smaller or lighter is cut down; everything that can be jettisoned is gone. Most song birds have eight or nine pairs of muscles, the sole function of which is to manipulate the syrinx, or song organ. That represents a fair commitment of resources. The syrinx, which sits atop the bird's airway, has been called something like a combination of our trachea and larynx, but really it is a unique construction of cartilage and membrane operated by the tugs and tilts of muscles and the pressure of the air that flows through it from the bronchial tubes.

The air, of course, is the prime maker of sound; the syrinx is a wind instrument. The membranes are the surfaces upon which the wind plays, vibrating as the air hits them on its way out from the lungs. The position of the membranes can be changed in many ways, as can the tautness of their surfaces. The airflow, too, can be manipulated—pushed in a tight column, fluffed in a wide breath, stuttered. Each modification produces a change in tone, pitch, volume, or rhythm.

Only humans command a vocal instrument with a greater range of effects. The bird has no vocal cords, as we do, and its mouth is not a sophisticated chamber in which the fundamental sound is modified into a precise final form. But the adjustability of the avian membrane-airflow

The hammerkop claims his bit of riverbank.

instrument matches much of the subtlety we gain from larynx and mouth, and surpasses us in several ways. Birds can sing more loudly than we, and can sustain their song without the muscular fatigue that keeps even the greatest diva's high notes brief. Because they don't shape their tones in the mouth, birds can sing with food, prey, or nesting material in their beaks, or with their beaks closed. And most amazingly, a bird can produce a different note from each bronchial tube at once—harmonizing with itself, singing in counterpoint, popping contrasting rhythms, all in a single breath and a single phrase.

We can figure out why birds bother with such arcane techniques if we look at ourselves. The subtleties of communication have become the basis for even our most elemental activities. Most action, instinctive or inventive, is a response to some choice; most choice is based on some communication sent or received. The more instinctive the action—that is, the less leeway it

allows for improvisation—the more limited the range of choice, and therefore the more important the slightest subtleties. In choosing a mate, a female kingbird hasn't a tremendous variety of options open to her. She's going to choose a male kingbird, she's going to choose one on this piece of turf or a plot nearby, and she's going to choose him right away. So the slight swell this guy gives to his mating song, and its rushed rhythmic quality, in contrast to the thinness of tone and dull foursquare beat of that fellow's peal, swings the choice.

Birds need territory, mates, offspring, and food. The quest for and maintenance of these things involve communication, and vocalization is obviously the bird's best way of communicating.

Ornithologists designate two types of bird song: call and song. Calls are usually brief exclamations, spontaneously uttered, arising from the immediate situation in which a bird finds itself. Calling is the moment-to-moment speech of birds,

Serenade: this male yellow-rumped caieque sings to the female inside the nest.

the way in which they say such things as, "Hey, here's some blackberries over here!" or "Where *are* you guys in this fog?" or "There's not room in this tree for both of us," or "Help!" or "Hey kids—come to dinner."

All birds have some kind of call, even if it is a rudimentary squawk used for warning and loving alike. Most birds have a larger vocabulary than that; several passerines make more than 20 kinds of noises, each with its own import.

The differences between the various calls of one bird may be great. Other birds make many calls that vary more subtly one from the other, and yet are clearly understood. The members of one species in one area are likely to use pretty much the same vocabulary, though calls will possibly vary a bit from those used by members of the same species in a different locale. Of course, calls vary from individual to individual in small ways. The personal touch is not as great as it is in song; one of the definitive requirements of a call is that it be interpreted immediately, often as a matter of urgency. If a cat is coming, it's no time to make artistic statements; it's time to holler "Hey! Cat!" and bolt.

Naturally, calls vary greatly from species to species. What is *wheet!* to a plover may be *pee-teer-rrreee* to a kingbird and *cut-cut-turrr* to a marsh wren. Each species has its own construction of the vocal apparatus—in fact, the layout of syrinx and attendant muscles is often used as a taxonomic key—and thus its own sonic capability. A marsh wren probably couldn't say *wheet!* if it tried, because it lacks not only the evolutionary tendency to use that locution, but also the right setup of membranes.

Nevertheless, there is at least one emergency in which birds may drop their differences in an inspiring show of avian esperanto. A researcher in England noted that different species used the same soft bleat to warn of the approach of a hawk, as if they had declared this sound to be an international code. The similarity of the "Hawk!" cry between these species is incredible, given the usual differences of their voices. It may

not be entirely due to the spirit of emergency brotherhood, however; the cry is a particularly good one in that it is audible but hard to place—that is, a bird uttering it does not give away its position, as it might with a more piercing or booming call. It may be that one species evolved this cry and kept surviving the surveillance of hawks, and others adapted themselves to the innovation.

Calls are instinctive; instinct is not usually what we look for to gather evidence of a creature's relative creativity and intelligence. Yet, because calls communicate with us as well as with other birds, we can see in their usage clear signs of analysis and decision. For example, the domestic rooster, famous for its daybreak *cock-a-doodle*, uses one alarm call, *gogogogok*, for danger approaching on foot, and another, *raaaay*, for danger in the sky. And why not? If there were only one alarm, a bird responding to it would have to guess where the foe was and choose the right means of hiding. If it guesses the threat is airborne, it will run to cover; if it guesses the threat is on the ground, it will fly. A wrong guess might deliver it right to the predator. The distinctive call, however, indicates the correct action. Similarly, many species of small birds have two responses to large birds spotted while the flock is engaged in foraging: the sentry issues an alarm cry, which sends the flock scattering, or a rallying cry, which brings the birds into a mob to harass the owl or hawk or crow.

Not all calls are for warning, of course. Baby birds, the most instinctive singers of all, cry for food, stimulating their parents to the task of getting and delivering it. Anyone who has been around a nest with new birds in it will be amazed to think that such calls are periodic; it certainly seems that they are issued all day long and that parents must be constantly aware of the need to stuff the little ones. However, an experiment with chaffinches revealed that the incessant chatter indeed serves a purpose. Adult chaffinches in captivity were surgically deafened (through the removal of the cochlea in the ear) and left to go about their lives in a colony of normal birds of their kind. The experiment was intended to study whether or not the deaf birds would continue to sing (they did, without impairment, for years). But what occurred as a side effect revealed the necessity of begging cries: the young of the deafened birds were inadequately fed and died, while the chicks of the other birds in the colony thrived at a normal rate.

The importance of begging cries also can be seen in species such as the brown pelican, turkey vulture, double-crested cormorant, and magnificent frigate bird. These birds are essentially mute as adults—but their young clamor in full voice, for feeding.

Many calls are simply location notes, expressions of identification and placement that request no more active response than a like utterance from nearby birds. Birds in a flock use chirps or peeps or *willit-willit*s to keep in touch, especially during migration or a group search for food, as needed. Species that spend a lot of time in brush and forest use the notes more than those living in open spaces, where visibility is unobstructed. Horned larks flying and walking over flat fields can see each other, so they do not need to call; rufous-sided towhees, which scratch in the dense ground cover of woods, call frequently, because they can see no farther than the pipsissewa or juniper around them.

In the case of especially elusive birds, ornithologists use recorded calls to evoke location notes that give away hiding places. The tape player has become a common tool of the field researcher looking for nocturnal birds, hidden nests, or rare species. Perhaps the saddest sonic quest of the past forty years is the search in southern Louisiana for the ivory-billed woodpecker, once our largest woodpecker, lord of the dense wetland forest. None have been seen in twenty years, but people still creep into the tiny part of its habitat that has not been logged and play its call into the silent gloom of the bayous. Reports of an answer are the most exciting news in American birddom.

Location notes are sometimes uttered purely in the service of fondness and the anxiety the loved one feels for the mate out of sight. The bienteveo tyrant bird of South America uses such a call even at the expense of its hunting. The male and female are both good hunters and search for prey separately among the fields and ponds of the pampas (the tyrant bird is something of an omnivore, relishing frogs, fish, insects, nestling birds, snails, and mice, all of which it can catch and kill). They agree to meet from time to time at a particular place. But after a while, one of the birds will grow lonesome and take a perch in the meeting ground, from which it will issue a piercing note. The other bird, though it may be hot on the trail of prey—or, worse yet, may be waiting silently for a mouse to show from beneath the grass—answers immediately with the same note. The lonesome bird keeps calling every minute, and the dutiful hunter keeps answering, until it has completed its task or reached the appointed time for the reunion with its mate. Then it flies back to the perch, joins the impatient one, and together, with crests raised, breasts puffed, and wings beating, they cry in the same tones they used in separation, just as loud, just as longing.

Ovenbirds show the same joy upon being reunited, but their expression moves away from the call and into song. The formal distinction depends upon several features of the vocalization: song is more often a sequence of notes or phrases that can roughly be presumed to contain an element of melodic composition, as opposed to the brief shout of a call; song is used more ritually, often in very strict formats and situations, in contrast to the spontaneity of a call; song often communicates through symbolism, where calls tend to say what they mean.

The ovenbirds, compared to the tyrant birds, demonstrate some of the differences. Like the bienteveos, the ovenbird mates forage separately and meet several times during the day to refresh their ardor. The waiting bird sees its mate coming and trills a song of clear single notes. The arriving bird joins the song, and immediately the first singer shifts to three-note figures, accenting the one and three. The second bird alights and matches the song, note for note, accent for accent. After a passionate duet passage the first bird drops out, and the second finishes with a solo coda of several increasingly strident notes.

There are many variations, from couple to couple, and even in successive meetings of the same couple, though the general format remains the same, as do the evident feelings.

This brings out a key feature of song: as consistent as its form may be within a species or a single individual, it is almost always a structure upon which marvelous improvisations are wrought. Song may be more ritualistic than calls, but it has its element of spontaneity, too—it allows for the creative expression of the feelings of the moment.

These feelings are fully measured in the song of the male at the beginning of the breeding cycle. The male sets himself up on a clear perch in territory he has selected as his fiefdom for the season, and he performs the richest song of his life. It is a proclamation of everything he has to offer a mate: strength, beauty, land, confidence that no male who hears him will challenge his dominion, and power to face any challenge that does come. Nowhere else in the animal world do we find such a holistic statement of self. Nowhere do we see such openness integrated with such brash posturing. It is a ritual bred in the bone, yet its message is passionately individual. To see a small sparrow standing on a branch, trilling and whistling in a voice 50 times its size, ready for all comers in love or war, dignified but cocky (it's where the word comes from, after all)—it is enough to make even the least bird-loving listener want to fly to his side. Female sparrows have the privilege of doing so.

The nature of the song's performance can make the difference between a bird that secures its prime land and strong mate, and a bird that is chased away to the lower forty and left alone.

All males of a species in a certain area have the same fundamental song, acquired through instinct and imitation. What they do with the common melody is what declares their power. It is not true that ornateness alone is sufficient, or even volume, though singing loud enough to be heard at the borders of your land is necessary. The females of different species respond to different qualities of singing with varying enthusiasm. And it must be admitted that the main feature they are listening for is simply male presence on good land.

Once a female has chosen a mate, however, the song that won her is still critical to her plans. She wants to build her nest, mate, lay her eggs, and rear her babies; all of these things depend on the male's ability to hold onto her and his plot of ground. Song is the first defense. A potential invader hears a strong song and moves on; if something in the song shows weakness, he may try to dislodge the singer. Field researchers have demonstrated this in several ways. Surgically muted male birds released onto their territory have found themselves under constant invasion—whatever their physical prowess, they couldn't keep the competition away because they couldn't sing. In another study, good turf upon which no claimant had yet arrived was "defended" by recorded song played through loudspeakers, and no other birds attempted to settle there.

Once the couple has joined, the male's proclamation song usually tails off in its frequency—the wood warbler, for example, will go from singing every minute or so to singing every five to ten minutes—and for some species a new, intimate song comes into play. The mating song is part of the male's courtship ritual, which may feature flashy flying, the display of grandiose feather configurations (crests, tail fans), ritual postures, dancing, gymnastics, and even architecture (see box on Nests for Show). The song is usually integrated with one of these activities, which inspire ritual responses in the female, leading eventually to a kind of pursuit game,

Durable, Not Disposable

It is often said that birds live *intensely* compared to mammals, especially humans: they pack so many more heartbeats, meals, travels, and family generations into their relatively brief lives. One reflection of this is the habit most passerines have of building nests as if they were going to occupy them for decades, then deserting them after a month or two.

A pair of mockingbirds or orioles wouldn't understand the "disposability concept" of, say, paper clothes: their instincts demand a well-made construction, not something that falls apart the day after it has served their needs. So the woods are full of rugged little woven cups, and the dead trees are hollow with nursery chambers of yesteryear.

The seasonal replication of such durable structures would seem wasteful of energy if not downright litterish, were it not for the many species of birds that use existing nests instead of building their own each year. There are three main groups of inquilines: those who reuse nests they themselves built earlier, those who reuse abandoned nests built earlier by other birds, and those who forcefully evict other birds from newly occupied nests.

Eagles and ospreys reuse their shaggy nests year after year, freshening them up each spring by piling new sticks onto the old. Sometimes the weight or volume accrues to the point that the original supports are overburdened, and the whole shebang collapses. But sometimes the nests last for decades: a famous osprey nest in

---

a chaste "engagement" in some species, and, finally, copulation.

The rituals have several purposes. First of all they allow the birds to verify beyond doubt that they are of the same species, an assurance craved by the universal instinct to resist hybridization. A suitor with moves different from those the female knows in her genes to be right for her kin, or a fiancée who greets a certain strut with an inappropriate wing beat, are rejected. The courtship ritual is a final test for both birds to prove their pedigree. In a function more specific to the feelings of the particular pair, the performance establishes the bond between them—after all, it is in most cases the first thing they do together—and demonstrates a more focused ardor that will eventually warm the female to connubial activities.

Usually the next thing they do together is select a nest site within the territory the male has established, and begin building a nest.

Just as birds' ability to fly gives them access to a great range of food items, so it gives them access to a fabulous range of homesites. In choosing a nesting place, a pair of birds responds to many imperatives of instinct covering everything from general environment (shady part of hillside forest) to specific locus (crotch between two twigs 40 to 45° apart and situated at least 30 feet above the ground on a hemlock limb), from an interior concept of ideal shape to a very practical sense of the properties of local materials. Each species has its own instincts for nesting, of course, just as it has its own feather colorations and diet.

One reason the contrast between nests is so

New England was used by a pair of birds for forty-four consecutive years. One peregrine falcon nest on a ledge in Great Britain has been in continuous seasonal use since Elizabethan times (which we know about thanks to continuous seasonal observation by generations of bird watchers). Among passerines, barn swallows and mourning doves tend to use their former nests, at least as foundations for new construction. The Gila woodpecker, which digs out a chamber in a giant saguaro cactus, often returns for a few years.

Most owls, titmice, chickadees, nuthatches, and several swallows use holes or crannies excavated by other birds. These species are the beneficiaries of woodpeckers, which dig new holes for their own broods each spring. Most of the inquilines do not return to the particular holes they occupy for a season, which leaves them open for new tenants; perhaps the only thing that keeps a woodpecker hole from being occupied for as long as an osprey nest is the fact that it is cut into a dead tree, which is probably growing less stable year by year.

Perhaps no bird is so victimized by nest pirates as the ovenbird of South America. Its nests are undeniably attractive: fully enclosed balls of adobe mud, stout and snug as the earthenware "oven" from which the bird derives its name. Yellow-throated sparrows and purple martins often boot the ovenbirds out as soon as the unfortunate laborers have finished their nest; then they proceed to fight each other for tenancy. Martins nest in all kinds of enclosures, usually in colonies; the sparrow usually bores into mud walls in South American towns and builds there. The ovenbird's domicile is obviously just right for both.

startling—and one reason the study of nests is so wonderful as a way of appreciating avian diversity—is that all nests serve basically the same purpose. With few exceptions, nests are for raising offspring in. The offspring begin childhood as eggs and end it as fledglings; in between, the parents provide the nest as a place to be incubated, nurtured, and protected from predators and weather.

Why, then, does an ostrich indifferently scrape a shallow depression in the earth while a hummingbird spins a geometrically perfect cup of stolen spider web decorated with lichen? Why does a wren sneak into the pocket of a tweed jacket on a hook, while the oriole knits and purls a hanging sack of grass and string? If all of them need only to keep their eggs warm, why the varying architecture? Why isn't there some proto-nest that all birds share an urge for?

Because there is no proto-bird, no proto-environment, no proto-life-style. A tufted titmouse does not think of his nesting instinct as something he has in common with his avian fellows; he thinks only of *his* immediate need to build on *this* spot out of *these* materials something that looks right to *him*, so *his* mate can lay some eggs and hatch some babies. Nesting is specific in time and place. As with all aspects of this annual cycle of breeding, the actions triggered by instinct happen anew each year—even when a pair of birds has mated for life, or when an old nesting site is used.

Nesting gives humans a chance to see—hence appreciate—the bird's instinct and adaptable intelligence. Subtler accomplishments are often less accessible to us: we cannot notice when a king-

Nests for Show

In many species, a male bird who has drawn a female to his territory tries to impress her by showing her around potential nest sites. This is an important part of the precourtship appraisal. The male is demonstrating not only his machismo at holding prime land, but also his awareness of familial responsibility. The female rewards such thoughtfulness by accepting the offer, mating, and eventually selecting one of the sites for a nest.

Some birds are not content merely to show *sites*, however. Several species of wren take the demonstration to a higher level of showmanship, going so far as to build the shells of enclosed nests at several locations. To leave time for the construction of their fantasy kingdoms, the male wrens arrive at the breeding grounds far ahead of the females. Each chooses his turf, then gets busy. A marsh wren or house wren will build as many as six "dummy nests," which he will show to a prospective mate as if he were a realtor. The female may select one of the dummies, in which case she will move in and finish the nest by lining it. Or she may acknowledge the male's nests as pure symbols, and pick another site for a new, completed nest.

Building six nests alone without the certainty of a mate is arduous enough, but the marsh wren happens to be polygamous *and* habituated to rearing many clutches of offspring per breeding season per mate. In the course of his three-month fertility, he may build 30 nests. It can happen that he attracts a full coterie of mates but occupies none of these model homes, except for leading fledglings to them for one-night stays between the real nest and the real world. It is clear, however, that the dummy nests are tremendously useful: males who build more of them attract more females.

The male bowerbird of Australia and New Guinea builds only one construction, but it is usually far more spectacular than any six wren nests. At the beginning of the breeding season, the bowerbird clears a large area and erects a spectacular structure that is ornately decorated with moss, leaves, bits of cloth or plastic, bottle caps, pieces of glass, ferns, shells, insect carapaces—almost anything that meets his high standards of beauty in color or shape. This structure becomes his parade ground: he leads an appraising female there and performs a wonderful array of struts, dances, and postures

---

fisher begins eating invertebrates once its creek dries up, or a sparrow varies its song in a particular mountain environment, using fewer notes and higher pitch because echo sends back interference.

We can observe the nest of a long-tailed tit more easily by parting the leaves of a hawthorn hedge: a perfect domed oval of moss, cobwebs, lichens, and hair woven together with a delicacy worthy of Fabergé, lined with a couple of thousand feathers, tightly constructed, perfectly attached to its supports, sculpturally beautiful and—best of all—functional. There are babies inside; they are warm; the foxes that patrol the area haven't been able to get at them. Or the sprawling cushion built by the pied wagtail made of grass strands, grass seed heads, moss (several kinds), lichens, horsehair, cattle hair, sheep wool,

Romance through architecture. (male satin bowerbird)

worthy of a mime, for which he is well-equipped with handsome plumage. If she is sufficiently impressed by both the bower and the bird, she accepts his advances and they copulate on the spot.

There are 18 species of bowerbird, and many types of bowers. Some are simply mats or platforms, 5 to 8 feet in diameter. Others are poles of woven twigs rising from moss foundations. Some birds build such a "maypole" with several uprights 10 feet high, roofed, and with trailing streamers. Others erect "avenues," walkways with walls on the sides, like something between a throne and a chamber, in which the the female stands to watch the male's performance. The satin bowerbird, which builds an avenue, decorates it with any object he can find that bears the bright blue color of his striking eyes. He also paints the bower's interior walls with a piece of bark he has steeped in a solution of berry pulp, saliva, and charcoal, to create a blue pigment.

Like some of the wren dummies, the bowers are not used for nesting; unlike the wren, however, the male bowerbird is not trying to impress the female with his potential domesticity. The bowers, like the courtship dances, are purely for show.

string, tin foil, seeds, twigs, feathers, conifer needles, plastic twine. If we were given a week to wander the wagtail's fiefdom and try to turn up the same selection of materials, we'd find it quite a job.

We can appreciate the job, because a nest is something *built* from scratch. It doesn't exist already in the bird—like hunger or voice—and in most cases it doesn't exist in nature. These fabulous objects were made, one by one, step by step, by individual birds.

The first of the ingenuities to be appreciated is the choice of site. As with most aspects of nesting, the selection of a specific spot is a matter of instinct. A chickadee knows it wants to scoop out the top of a dead tree stump, while the swift heads for the eaves of a building, and the ancient murrelet looks for places to burrow between

Communal and Dump Nests

Brood parasitism is not the only way to cut corners on the labor of building nests and incubating. A few species establish communes, in which several females lay their eggs in a single nest and all of the adults in the families take turns incubating. Nests of the smooth-billed ani have been found containing 29 eggs; of the groove-billed ani, containing 15; and of the acorn woodpecker, containing 10.

The females of several species of pheasant, duck, and gallinule will lay into a single nest without bothering to establish a commune first—they simply dump their eggs and abandon them. Usually these are hens who have not yet built nests of their own. Once an egg is formed it must be laid, and the hen bearing it evacuates it into the container she is instinctively drawn to, imposing her product on one of her cousins, who is otherwise fortunate enough to have a nest. A "dump nest" starts as a normal single-family dwelling, but once it is invaded the egg-burdened hens from the neighborhood flock to it, and soon it may be so packed that the original proprietor is forced to abandon it as so much sanitary landfill. The eggs are not incubated. A dump nest of redhead ducks was once found with 87 eggs in it.

Many wrens build nests in any kind of cavity.

rocks on northern shorelines. Each species has its literal niche. Individuals in environments that do not match the species' classic settings do adapt somewhat, but there is a remarkable consistency in site selection from one locale to the next.

Generally birds choose sites related first of all to their feeding habits. The bird spends most of its time in the environment in which it finds its food. This is naturally the element in which it is most comfortable and confident. The rufous-sided towhee, which scratches for insects in the underbrush of woods, builds a nest under bushes; the dipper, which lives and eats in and around mountain streams, builds a nest that is as close to a submarine as possible, sometimes under a waterfall; the soaring golden eagle, which spots large prey from on high, picks a ledge far up a cliff face for its nest.

The advantage of having your young in the same general area as your food source is clear: nestlings are hungry and must be fed dozens of time each day. Hunting or foraging is difficult enough for an adult bird without the added expenditure of energy required by a long transit from hunting ground to home.

Sometimes, of course, the very concept of a nest is incompatible with a feeding environment. Waterfowl must forsake their aquatic comforts for terra firma. Eggs must be kept warm and, for the most part, dry. So ducks, loons, gulls, terns, penguins, albatrosses, and murres move inland —usually only slightly—where they trade their marine elegance for awkward wobbling on feet ill-placed for long treks to find just the right reed or feather. Perhaps this is one reason many water birds build almost no nest at all, laying their eggs smack on stony beaches or bare rock ledges. Many of these species nest in colonies—some of them cooperative, some merely coexistent— going against the instinct for privacy seen in many landlocked passerine birds, but consistent with the urge to dump the eggs with a minimum of terrestrial activity. *Take as few steps as possible from the waterline and lay* seems to be the imperative here.

The grosbeak weaver with his handiwork.

Most ducks, geese, and swans build more commodious nests a bit more removed from the sea's uncertain edge; indeed, some duck nests, such as those of the eider, are models of comfort. This is largely because of the feathered lining, and here once again the waterfowl shows a way of saving steps on the passerine. Where the long-tailed tit wanders far afield for the feathers of scores of birds—feathers shed in molts, broken in hunts, discarded by predators—to line its nest, the eider simply tucks its head and plucks down from its own richly layered breast. Eiders possess this down primarily because they need to insulate their bodies against the cold water in which they spend most of their lives, but the need for nest insulation close-at-beak is perhaps an evolutionary factor, too.

Grebe nests are leaky basements compared to the higher and drier apartments of the eider, but they have the advantage of being close to the action. These water birds build soggy floating platforms of vegetation (reeds, roots, and bottom plants), tether them to a plant on the bottom, and nest right on the raft. Jacanas—those fantastic lily-pad walkers—take advantage of their mobility to build floating nests, too, as do coots. Perhaps the most industrious commitment to a watery nest belongs to the horned coot, which lives around mountain lakes in the South American Andes. There is little vegetation in this en-

vironment, and the bird cannot count on the riot of reeds from which grebes select their building materials, or the bottom plants that allow luckier birds to secure their nests. So the horned coot takes to the mountains and becomes a miner. Carrying back stones one by one—sometimes as heavy as a pound—it builds a huge mound on the bottom of its pond until the cone-shaped pile reaches just below the surface of the water. Then, on this incredible foundation, it builds its nest of water plants, not terribly different in appearance from the nursery of the relatively lazy grebe. Perhaps "horned coot's nest" should become a metaphor to replace the overused "tip of the iceberg."

Birds who spend most of their lives on the wing, are in the same dilemma as waterfowl: they must abandon their element to settle down on a nest. Swifts and swallows and nightjars rarely

The eider plucks its breast to insulate its nest, a concept to which winter-jacket manufacturers owe a lot.

The pie-billed grebe's egg is afloat in its nest.

touch down during the non-breeding seasons. They are weak afoot—most are very poor even at perching. They gather all of the airborne insects they eat in flight. Everything about their design suggests an aerial life, just as the features of a loon demand water. But nests cannot be built in the air.

The air birds, as we might designate them, show a greater variety in their choice of "displaced" nesting sites than waterfowl. In the swallow family alone, cliff and cave swallows build mud nests on sheer stone, bank swallows burrow into riverbanks, tree swallows find holes in hollow tree trunks, rough-winged swallows assemble twiggy things in drainpipes or gutters, and barn swallows stick mud and straw cups under eaves in dark buildings.

Whippoorwills seem to feel that nothing they built could be as perfectly camouflaged as their bodies—so they plop their eggs directly onto the unmodified forest floor and hunker down over them, looking like bits of log and leaf. Nighthawks lay their eggs just as unceremoniously, but on gravel, often on the flat roofs of buildings. Swifts, even more aerial in life-style than swallows—tend to fasten skimpy half-cups of twigs or mud (or, in one species, hardened saliva) high on the walls of canyons, silos, barns, or hollow trees. These nests have in common a certain height and inaccessibility except by flight, which gives them a thematic link to the life of the birds when they were unburdened by parenthood.

The falcons who prey upon flying birds would

Partners in the Nest

Birds not only use nests built by other birds; sometimes they move into structures built by mammals, reptiles, or insects. The structures can be anything from burrows to anthills, occupied or vacated. In cases of mutual occupation, the host often gains something from the presence of the birds, but not always—and never, it seems, does it gain as much as the birds do.

In Africa and South America, many species, including trogons, kingfishers, puffbirds, and parrots nest in the huge mud cities of termites. These are sturdy structures that can easily be adapted to the birds' needs with a little hollowing-out and lining; they provide a kind of shelter the bird could not duplicate on its own. Some species choose abandoned termite nests, but others don't bother—they move right in with the insects, and the insects (one suspects begrudgingly) accept and ignore them.

Many tropical passerines build their nests near or within those of Hymenoptera— stinging wasps and bees. In a few cases, this is because the insect builds a strong structure of mud or papier-mâché and the bird envies its snugness. But most of the time the birds simply want to profit from the forbidding presence of the stinging bugs, which keep at bay such predators as toucans, snakes, and monkeys, who might snap up the eggs and chicks. Also, for reasons that have not been discovered, Hymenoptera repel a vicious tropical fly that is a major cause of death in chicks of many species. The birds can reciprocate by defending their nests—and by association, those of the insects—against advances by anteaters and caracaras (scavenging birds who

seem close to this aerial life, but compared to the swifts and swallows, most raptors must confess to a lot of commerce with the earth. They hunt creatures who dwell on its surface and often make their kills on the ground. The nests of the larger hawks and eagles, in contrast to the swifts' minimalist saucers, are sprawling snaggles of dead tree limbs of a size most passerines build their nests *upon*. Yet the raptors share with the aerial birds a yen for the high remove; the golden eagle's cliff-side aerie, or the red-tailed hawk's nest in a tall, lone tree echo the cave swallow's lofty little cup in spirit if not in form.

And in form there is certainly a contrast. The bald eagle builds the world's largest nest—or, rather, accumulates it—adding to it year after year until the massive platform is as much as 10 feet deep and 10 feet in diameter. The nest, built atop a tree, is used until it collapses from its own weight. In its unruly mass it resembles the osprey nest; but the osprey is less choosy than the eagle, casting its platform on almost any upright near the water it fishes: tree, fence post, telephone pole, windmill, sign post, billboard, chimney, even a floating buoy. (Ospreys are just as catholic in their materials, wedging bottles, fishnets, leather belts, rubber boots, clothing, cans, hats, and toys into their brambles. The novelist John Steinbeck examined an osprey nest in his garden and discovered three shirts, a bath towel, an arrow, and his own garden rake inside.)

Perhaps the nest most defined by its site is the hole: it's simply *there*, without even the illusion of portability that a construction creates. There will gladly eat a chick and a wasp in successive bites).

Birds rarely nest with mammals other than man. Two exceptions are the minera and the black-collared swallow of South America, who both inhabit secondary burrows dug off the main channels of holes occupied by an animal called the vizcacha. The vizcacha is a communal rodent, living in townships comprising many very large burrows. The swallow and minera become suburbanites, zipping in through the main entrances but quickly branching off into their own crannies, disturbing the rodents as little as possible. The birds obviously gain easy housing, and perhaps a small degree of protection by association with the rodents. It is not clear that the rodents gain anything, but they don't seem to mind.

Several species of swallow and swift nest primarily in human structures, as do barn owls. Wrens will build in anything from a boat to a bottle, even lining with grass the pocket of an old wool jacket or the cavity of a boot. A pair of wrens in a California office building built a rafter nest from pirated office supplies: pins, elastic bands, paper clips, thumbtacks, wire.

Nearly 50 bird species will move into birdhouses built specifically for them, and several others will occupy nest brackets or shelves placed on the walls of buildings. Most of the cavity-nesting birds will give a house a try. However, for the house to attract and keep a certain bird, the dimensions of everything from the entry hole to the floor size must match standards that ornithologists have devised for that species through observation and experiment. A few species, such as the eastern bluebird, have strengthened their breeding populations due to nationwide volunteer campaigns to place man-made houses outdoors for their use.

are many hole dwellers, especially among the passerines; some use existing cavities (natural crannies in rocks, hollows in logs or trees) and manufactured (disused rodent burrows), while some make their own.

Though the general rule of nesting in the environment of the food source is followed, the placement within that environment is often very odd. Kingfishers, who hunt from perches over water, build nests in muddy banks. They fly at the earth surface and deliver walloping pecks with their huge bills to begin the excavation; after that, they burrow (shoveling with the beak, scuffing dirt backward with the feet) until the upward-sloping tunnel reaches 3 to 6 feet, sufficiently removed from the world for an incubation chamber about a foot in diameter. The female lays the eggs on the bare earth, but the chamber and tunnel soon get a linoleum-like floor of slimy fish scales from food brought in to the chicks. Kingfisher nests are difficult to see, but easy to smell.

The pardalotes of Australia peck flowers for their nourishment—a daylight open-air life if ever there was one—but they too burrow into the ground to lay their eggs. They differ from the kingfishers and most other burrowing birds, however, in that they do not stop at excavation and rudimentary shaping of a terminal chamber. The pardalotes build nests of woven bark at the end of their tunnels—the spotted pardalote goes so far as to erect a fully domed structure, a room within a room.

Many of the tree dwellers build structures in-

Ospreys build craggy piles.

side their holes. Chickadees tend to dig in the soft tops of rotting tree stumps or trunks, whereas titmice and nuthatches use cavities that already exist; all of these birds then build interior nests, mostly of soft materials—moss, plant fibers, hair, and feathers—with some leaves and bark. Although red-breasted nuthatches use existing holes, they modify the openings by smearing pitch around them. This may be a kind of possessive marking to alert other hole hunters to the fact that the spot is taken. There is a premium on good holes in trees among the passerines who cannot chip wood themselves; in the spring, many of these birds scramble to take over occupied holes while the occupant is out gathering nesting material or food.

The birds who provide most of the up-for-grabs holes are, of course, the woodpeckers. All woodpeckers except the ground woodpecker of South Africa nest in substantial holes dug industriously in the trunks of trees. The trees are dead, at least at the heart; if you see a woodpecker hammering a tree you know to be fully alive, the bird is either looking for food or drumming for purely sonic effect. (The one exception to the dead-tree rule is the red-cockaded woodpecker, who digs nest holes in living pine trunks and intentionally sets resin flowing around the opening; it manages to get in and out without gumming up its feathers, but apparently parasites cannot manage this and are discouraged from intruding.)

Woodpeckers use their special bills (and their special shock-absorbing skulls) with gusto, once they have chosen a spot. A male great spotted woodpecker will flail away at the wood before him for six hours a day; black woodpeckers work as a team for even longer, with the female alternating with the male in one-hour shifts. That's a lot of woodchopping, but the woodpecker requires more than a tight squeeze—the cavities are generally quite spacious. The larger species, such as the pileated woodpecker, may dig out a chamber 2 to 3 feet deep.

Woodpeckers do not add nest materials to their handiwork, although they leave a layer of chips on the bottom of the new nursery. Excess chips are ejected from the hole and allowed to accumulate at the bottom of the trunk, or in some cases carted away. The whole excavation is a tremendous task, taking weeks of labor, yet woodpeckers almost always dig new holes for breeding each year. This leaves a lot of prime dwelling space for other birds—and sometimes squirrels or bats—to fight over. Some indwellers, especially starlings, will even try to roust woodpeckers directly after the hole is finished. Sometimes they succeed and the woodpecker must do the job again; but if the thieves are repelled, they will settle for a "used" bivouac.

The woodpecker's simple holes, for all of the work that distinguishes them from the tern's scratch in the sand, are nevertheless rather crude nests. It is in the passerines—perching songbirds, the largest avian order—that we find more elaborate discernment and action. Passerines are the fabulous *builders* of the avian world—indeed, of all nature—and in studying their nests we move into the field of amazing animal architecture.

Placement, of course, is the first choice of the passerine. Its instincts guide it to just the right spot as deliberately as do those of the eider or flicker. There is a wonderful relationship between locus and structure—the woven bag of the Bal-

The northern oriole weaves a tight bag.

timore oriole hanging delicately from the tip of a tiny branch too small for a predator to tread; the saliva-cemented cone of the hermit hummingbird, suspended from a light palm frond on a single thread so long that the bird cannot perch while building, but must daub from the air and, finally, counterbalance the asymmetrical thread with a long trailer beneath the cone; the

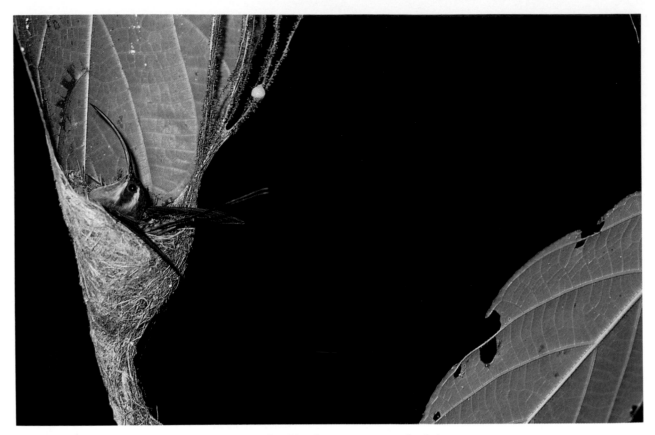

Just the spot: a long-tailed hermit hummingbird hitches its nest to a leaf tip with cobwebs.

fluffy cup of the tailorbird, protected from the tropical rain that would ruin its warmth by a canopy of living leaves to which it is literally stitched.

The instinct that leads the bird to a site is integrated with the instinct for its nest's design. The weaver bird does not find itself on the tip of a spiky palm leaf and say, "Let's see—maybe a two-chambered domed structure woven lightly out of long plant fibers, with a drooping sleeve for an entrance." It sets up house on the leaf tip because it knows exactly what kind of nest it must build. Most passerine nests are far more than what will work on a site. They involve niceties of design and construction—camouflage, extra protective devices, or features for comfort— that exceed the rudimentary requirements of the spot.

Once the site is selected, and the nest's design is in the bird's mind as a constant ideal, the bird must collect the materials it needs. The more complicated passerine nests are built in stages, each of which demands a series of materials specific to that stage—for example, a foundation of twigs, lined with mud and straw, then lined with wool and feathers, then capped with a grass dome, the outside of which is then all hung with moss and lichen. The selection and collection of this stuff, while doubtless inspired by species-wide instinct, requires a little more improvisation from the individual bird than other aspects of nesting.

One reason for this is that instincts do not necessarily keep step with the times. Horsehair used to be a common nesting material; when horses were all over town and country, a bird who felt the instinct for some hair could fly to a stable nearby and pluck it from a curry comb or harness, or to a pasture and yank it from a mane or tail. But horses are harder to find now. A chipping sparrow—which once used so much horsehair that it got the nickname "hairbird"—cannot fly 100 miles to locate a horse, in the midst of its nesting compulsion. Instead it will find some skinny grasses nearby, or some pine needles. Probably the instinct for horsehair will fade in time, as the species survives with substitutions. Birds adopt modern materials exactly as humans do; for example, where many birds used to use long grass strands or—if they were lucky enough to find it—yarn for weaving, some now use plastic twine or monofilament fishing line (which, being more prevalent than yarn was in the old days, would require even less good luck to find).

Another reason for improvisation: the material instincts of a species do not apply to all environments in which the birds may find themselves. Local substitutes replace ideals. The Gentoo penguin, a far-flung species, uses wood bits on South American islands, moss and seaweed in southern Georgia, and, inside the plantless Antarctic, animal substances such as bones and feathers. The urge to build a nest is always stronger than the drive to use a certain material. A bird will not go nestless for want of an item for which a substitute can be found—and it can prove to be very clever in the location of such substitutes.

Some birds are specially equipped with a primary material within themselves, which makes them simultaneously self-sufficient and self-dependent. We have seen how the eider, like many ducks, turns a crude platform into a comfy nest with its own down. Even more remarkable is the salivary equipment of the swifts, swallows, and martins, which produces a huge amount of adhesive fluid the birds use as mortar. Whether it is a chimney swift holding twigs together and fastening them to a wall, or a cliff swallow turning pellets of earth into bricks, the bird's dependence on its glandular superabundance is complete. Without

This lesser masked weaver has finished his chamber; now, upside down, he'll build a long, hanging sleeve as an exclusive entryway.

horsehair the "hairbird" will find grass. But what would the swift do without its saliva? The entire interior process of forming mud or fastening sticks held in the beak would have to become an exterior manipulation, almost as if a human suddenly had to chew food outside the body.

No such adaptation is likely to be required of the swift or swallow. Indeed, some species have

Minimalism: The African jacana lays its fine-art eggs right on the succulents and grasses; the oyster catcher throws a few shell fragments onto a plain of rocks; the fairy tern lays its single egg onto a bare tree limb, where it must be balanced throughout incubation.

gone even farther in the other direction, to utter independence from external materials: certain species of swiftlets in Southeast Asia build nests entirely from saliva. As with other swifts, the birds' salivary glands expand during breeding season. But instead of using the glutinous white stuff merely to complement the shape of twigs or mud balls, the swiftlets construct shallow half-cups from the effluvium, which hardens and holds shape. The cups are attached to the walls of the dark caves in which the birds live, sometimes as high as 300 feet up a sheer wall. An industry sprang up many years ago when someone discovered that the nests were edible (though tasteless), and that highfalutin' food merchants would pay well for the chance to float one in a bowl of chicken broth and serve it to a gourmand. The men of certain families became nest farmers, venturing into the Niah caves, which house per-

haps 2 million adult birds and, risking their lives daily, generation after generation, to climb bamboo poles hundreds of feet up in the dark recesses and slice hardened saliva away from the slippery walls.

Most birds, however, must find the nest materials out in the environment. The most commonly used vegetation products are twigs and branches, leaves, bark, rotten wood (made into a paste with saliva), moss, reeds, grasses, "plant down" from cottonwoods or milkweeds or thistles, lichens, seaweed, algae, seeds, and hulls. Animal products are just as useful, especially wool, hair, spider silk from webs, bones, snakeskin, regurgitated pellets from raptors, feathers, and eggshells. For most birds, these things serve precise purposes, and their use is worthy of an engineer; moss makes a superb insulator, for example, and the felt composed by the hum-

A Nest Fit for Poe

The hornbills of Africa, Asia, and Polynesia are revered in tribal societies and legally protected in several countries. The main reason is the bird's stunning beak: a thick, down-pointing scimitar topped, in most species, by a large casque. Hornbill skulls are worn as headdresses in tribal ceremonies, and the ivory of the casque, carved by craftsmen, is the main export of many societies.

The hornbill possesses a high mystique that has less to do with its bill than its nest, however. It is a nest right out of *The Cask of Amontillado*.

At the start of the breeding season, male and female hornbills select a tree cavity (or in a few cases, a slit between rocks) that will serve as their nest. Immediately, the female begins to seal the entry with muddy mortar. When only a small slit remains —just enough to allow her passage—she squeezes through into the dark interior and resumes her sealing work from the inside, now using her feces as plaster. She stops when only the tip of her beak can protrude.

The male brings food and nest-lining material, passing insects and fruit into her bill 25 to 30 times a day. She settles to the task of laying 1 to 5 eggs and incubating them for 25 to 40 days. When the chicks hatch, the male goes into high gear, bringing them food up to 70 times a day; the female feeds the young and uses their excrement to keep her seal strong, until the chicks are able to back up to the slit and expel their droppings, as she does.

In some hornbill species, the female breaks out at this point, taking several hours to hack her way through the cemented disk she was reinforcing just the day before. The nestlings immediately repair the damage she has wrought, using their feces and sticky fruit passed in by the male parent. When the seal is nearly complete, the chicks stop and both parents feed them for 40 to 80 days through the tiny hole. The young bird breaks its own way out when it is ready to fly; later fledglings reseal the chink after each departure, so each one gets a chance to crash through the wall.

Other species allow no such departure for the female; she remains inside for the duration of incubation and fledging. She takes advantage of her captivity to molt completely, safe from such predators as snakes that would worry her in this vulnerable condition. When she finally breaks out, she is ready in every way to fly off. So are the young who will never return to the nest.

mingbird of spider silk and thistle down is ethereally light, soft, and strong. Some birds use odd substances purely for decoration—hawks keep fresh sprigs of green leaves in the nest, for example, replacing them as they go brown—but most have at least the purpose of decorative camouflage in mind, such as that provided by lichens or bark attached to the outermost surface of the nest.

Once the materials have been gathered, the building begins. As with the seizure and ingestion of food, the bird uses its physical tools with dexterous versatility. In addition to the bill and feet, birds use other parts of their bodies—breast,

The wandering albatross picks a room with a view.

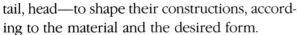
Togetherness: Sociable weavers build condominiums, while Adelie penguins are alone in a crowd.

tail, head—to shape their constructions, according to the material and the desired form.

The most common type of construction is the cup nest. Birds of all sizes build them in all environments, but the sequence of assembly usually follows a common pattern. First, with its beak (and sometimes a scrabble from the foot) the bird builds a platform on the ground or a ledge, or attached to a tree branch. Next, it roughly shapes the exterior bowl, refining the surface in succeeding "drafts" by tucking loose ends of grass or bark, or securing them with filament, or plastering them; this, too, is a task for the bill. The interior cup is then perfected, whether it is composed of added material (mud, feathers, wool, leaves) or is simply the inner surface of the fundamental material, by a wonderful spinning action of the female: she sits inside the cup, with her wings tucked and her feet beneath her, and

presses her arching breast against the cup, rotating again and again until the circular smoothness is satisfactory all around her. The interior is taut, snug, and beautifully round. She will be comfortable there, keeping her eggs as much as 45° warmer than the surrounding air; her babies will find it a comfortable home, too.

Hanging nests are usually woven of subtler material—strands of grass, reeds, and fibers, rather than patches of moss or bark—and thus require an amazing deftness of bill (and neck). Lightness is critical; the structures are often hung from the most fragile of twigs or leaves. Some of these nests are so delicate as to be almost transparent, such as the spider-silk baskets of some hummingbirds and the grass-thread bags of the weaverbirds. A nest suspended in space is accessible only from the air, which removes it from the reach of many terrestrial and arboreal predators. However, it may require aerial construction work, as performed by some hummingbirds who build from a constant hover. With others, such as the weaver, the first component

Echo

Two cave-dwelling birds—the oilbird of northern South America and the cave swiftlet of Southeast Asia—have songs they sing not to mates, not to competing males, not to their young, but only to themselves. Both of these birds find their way in their dark environment by echolocation: the emission of sounds that bounce back and reveal the contours of their surroundings.

This is similar to the techniques of bats and old submarines, but unlike bats the birds use midrange frequencies audible to humans; we hear their songs as a series of sharp clicks. The oilbird, which eats fruit, and the insectivorous swiftlet do not use their sonar to find food, as bats do. The oilbird flies out of its cave at night and sees well enough to feed itself. The swiftlet apparently sees its prey, too, when it hunts in parts of its caverns that are dimly illuminated by daylight filtering in from the distant outdoors. Neither bird utters its periodic clicking when there is light enough for it to see where it is going. Experiments with a captive oilbird showed that when its ears were temporarily sealed and it flew in a dark room, it ran into the walls.

erected—once a strand of grass or string has been wound around or knotted to the support—is a work perch that will serve as a kind of scaffolding, eventually to be assimilated into the form of the nest. Weavers, tailorbirds, and orioles are the Brussels lacemakers of the avian world, able to tat, stitch, baste, weave, and, in some cases, even to tie half-hitches with their bills. One field observer watched a Baltimore oriole through the whole process of building its nest and estimated that in the course of more than 40 hours of work the bird had taken 10,000 stitches and tied several thousand knots.

Many hanging nests go beyond the simple cup shape and are fully domed, with lush interiors. Many are even more ornately designed, with trapdoors, fake entrances, and multiple chambers. Such features have probably evolved as refinements of protection, taking the concept of protection beyond the purely physical into the realm of perception and analysis. The African kapok tit hangs its domed nest in a tree, with a slit for entry near the point of attachment. The departing bird gives this slit a peck, and the opening vanishes. However, beneath it is a larger hole, left open and clearly visible. This entry leads only to an empty space; a predator intruding here might conclude the nest was deserted, and depart.

There are several species of weaverbird, building several kinds of nests—all of them beautifully finished. The most ingenious and spectacular are those containing an egg chamber that can be reached only through an antechamber, which in turn can be reached only through a long entry tube hanging downward from the globe of the nest like a sleeve from a jacket. These nests can be entered by the bird alone and only through a special aerobatic maneuver. The weaver approaches the nest, drops into a deep dive, whips itself upward toward the end of the tube, tucks its wings, and lets its carefully calculated (and aimed) momentum carry it up through the narrow tunnel to the threshold of the antechamber. Even the craftiest tree snake couldn't manage to penetrate here.

In most species, nest building is cooperative work. (great blue herons)

Many ornithologists equate complexity of nest construction with longevity of evolution—that is, they believe birds such as the weaver and tit are more highly evolved than crude devil-may-care sand scratchers—the tern, plover, and nighthawk. This supposes that survival has required a constant expansion of technique in these passerines, a complex inventiveness leading to a compulsion for the rococo. Other theorists disagree, saying the non-builders demonstrate a principle of nature no less brilliant than the devices of invention: the path of least action leads to evolution. If the plover keeps thriving by dumping its eggs on the bare beach generation after generation, why should it feel compelled to demonstrate its evolutionary progress by getting into crenellation? Activity is to be kept to a minimum; energy should always be reserved for the securing of food; if a couple of seashells nudged into a rough semicircle serve just as well as a bag requiring 10,000 stitches, why take unnecessary pains?

The issue will probably not be resolved on the consideration of survival only; the purpose of ornate nests takes us into the realm where instincts and hormones keep their ageless secrets. It is clear that in many passerines the female needs to see some fancy nestwork before she submits to copulation; perhaps the male builder is simply carrying out the obligations of courtship, offering symbolic protection against dangers long moot in the world but still recalled in the genetic subconscious of the species, like a man of today walking on the outside of a woman in the street (so she won't be splashed by the wagons passing in the mud streets of Boston or Los Angeles).

The point of nest-building, ultimately, is that it leads a female to feel secure in depositing her eggs and raising her offspring—it leads, in other words, to survival of the species. There is no doubt that this is the ultimate goal of every behavior of every animal on the earth.

The Fast Family

Of all egg-layers—and that means most of earth's creatures, including insects, fish, reptiles, and one mammal (Australia's platypus)—birds have evolved the most rarified treatment of their eggs after laying. Most creatures, even those who build crude nests, lay their eggs and leave them. The hatchlings are born with the physical ability and instinct to strike boldly out into the world, where most of them are immediately eaten by predators, but where a few will find the means to survive. Thirty years ago, a popular nature film showed us the labor and delivery of a sea turtle, dragging her bulk up the beach on awkward flippers, digging a hole into which she dumped her 40 or so eggs in the course of a long night, hauling her considerably lightened bulk back to the surf, and washing out to sea like a deflating raft, with exhaustion and relief. Every parent in every theater in America was wowed by the dedication and pluck of this Supermom; her collapse into the safety of the waves was greeted with cheers of admiration. The film then rather cursorily showed the hatching of the tiny baby turtles, who had been left underground without food with 60 yards of beach to traverse on much tinier and less-practiced flippers, in brilliant daylight, under the hungry eyes of terns and gulls. The babies dug themselves out, blinked with matinal optimism, stretched their flippers, and sprinted for the surf. I recall —as a six-year-old—nearly missing amid the laughter the narrator's murmured comment that most of them, alas, would be gobbled up before they got their noses wet.

Birds treat their young better than this—much more as we do, with solicitation and total support. The young need it from the time they are ensconced in a shell to the time they finally stretch their wings and take off. Some species produce precocious chicks, but no baby bird could sprint across 60 yards of sky at the age of one hour. It's often difficult enough just getting out of the shell.

Getting into the shell is easier: birds have a strong reproductive system and high fertility performance. Oddly enough, the most ineffi-

Facing page: Herring gull egg.

Fairy terns do everything *elegantly.*

cient moment seems to be the initial one, the coition that introduces the male's sperm into the female's body. Evolution has not smiled on the avian penis—the only birds that retain them (ostriches, a few ducks, and gallinules) are regarded as rather lowly evolved. So, instead of injecting the sperm neatly into the female's sexual cavity, the male bird mounts his mate (often literally, standing on her back) as she skews her tail out of the way, presses his cloaca against hers—this is "the cloacal kiss"—and releases a flow of semen.

Perhaps the main reason this works so well is that bird semen is astoundingly potent. With the advent of breeding season the testes swell about *50,000 percent*, and the expanded tissue is far from idle: a bird will release up to 4 billion spermatozoa in a single ejaculation (compared to about 400 million from a human). The sperm make their way up the female's oviduct—a channel running from cloaca to ovary—and meet the ovum. The tadpole-like sperm are fleet: in domestic fowl fertilization may take place 25 minutes after copulation.

Once the egg is fertilized, it continues its progress down the oviduct, which now demonstrates that it is much more than a mere passageway. With its five chambers, it is more like a series of craftsmen's shops that will turn the tiny ovum into a polished egg full of nourishment enough to see it through its growth, self-sufficient in its fundamental protection. The muscles of the oviduct conduct the ovum down in stages, leaving it in each passage long enough to acquire albumen, shell membranes, shell, and pigment. By the time the egg reaches the vagina to be laid—as soon as 24 hours after copulation in some birds—the ovum (now the yolk) is im-

These bald eagles mate outside the nest, but well in sight of it.

The male roadrunner brandishes the lizard as a trophy signifying his worthiness to mate and provide for a family.

mersed in four layers of albumen, stabilized by a pair of cords within the albumen's fluid so that it will always orient correctly no matter what the egg's position, surrounded by two membranes that separate it from the shell leaving an airspace at one end, and finally sealed inside a hard mineral shell.

The makeup of the egg's meat varies. In passerines, most of whose hatchlings are utterly helpless—blind, featherless, unable to regulate body temperature—the yolk is about 20 percent of the egg's weight. In species whose hatchlings are better equipped for immediate action—with feathers, open eyes, and a sense of self-determined mobility—the yolk is larger, taking up from 35 to 50 percent of the egg.

The shell is mostly calcium carbonate; about 60 percent of the calcium comes from food eaten by the mother bird, with the rest derived from the tissue of her large bones. Thickness varies from species to species. Birds who are rougher with their eggs, birds who live in harder environments, and birds who do not provide cushy nests tend to produce eggs with thicker shells. The francolin makes the world's heavyweight champion of eggshells, using 28 percent of the egg's weight just in the coating; the ground nests of this pheasant-like bird are subject to heavy predation on the steppes of Africa. Dove eggs, continuously incubated and thus less exposed to danger or rough handling, have very thin shells.

Shell thickness can vary within the composition of a single egg, according to how the egg is treated. Guillemot eggs are laid on rocky ledges and have a characteristic shape, much more pointed at one end, so that an egg jostled into motion will roll in a circle instead of in a straight line—off the ledge. At their pointed ends—those that rotate against the rock—they are thick, while their broad ends—which do not touch anything—are thin. The broad end is also where the chick emerges. Many bird shells are thinner in the area the chick has to break. All shells are porous, allowing an exchange of carbon dioxide and oxygen through the surface.

One bird's egg has an extra protective layer: the grebe, with its floating nest of watery weeds, often gets its eggs wet—so it lays them with a waxy cuticle covering the shell.

The color of an egg determines its visibility to parents, hosts, and predators, and thus is very important. Woodpeckers, owls, and other birds

There are four eggs here, from (left to right) an extinct elephant bird, whose eggs are unearthed from time to time; an ostrich, largest egg among living birds; a domestic fowl; and a hummingbird, whose eggs are the world's smallest.

Cuckoos can produce eggs (on the right in each pair) that mimic those of the hosts whose nests they parasitize.

that nest in dark holes have white eggs, which are easier for the parents to see in the darkness. They also require no camouflaging coloration, so coloration is foregone, in line perhaps with an evolutionary law that says no unnecessary feature should be perpetuated in a bird's life or products.

Camouflage is critical for many other species. The shorebirds who build no nest but lay directly on the beach, rocks, or shingle produce eggs that blend right into the pebbles and shells around them. Nighthawk eggs are speckled to resemble the pattern of the gravel upon which they are laid. The grouse's egg is a splotchy dark brown, perfectly imitative of the leafy floor of its woodland habitat.

The colors of other eggs are more difficult to explain—the coffee brown of the loon's, the glossy black of the emu's, the rich blue of the heron's. Generally the color of the egg is consistent within a species, especially within a particular environment. But there are exceptions —murre eggs often vary in color in a colony on a single ledge! One bird's egg (murres lay only one) will be cream-colored, the next will have chocolate splashes, and a third will be gray, streaked with brown. The different colors may be a way for the sets of parents to identify their particular egg in the jumble of colonial life.

When a ground-laying species is spread through environments with widely different coloration, the eggs in one location may be quite different from those in another; the birds are able to adapt their mechanisms of pigmentation to mimic the local colors. No adaptation is as flexible as the European cuckoo's, however. It is able to imitate in both size and pigment the eggs of the species into whose nest it puts its eggs (see boxed text on Brood Parasitism).

Once the eggshell has its pigment it is ready to be laid. This momentous step, of course, simply fits into the overall pattern of the reproductive cycle, all of which is directed by hormonal activity, which in turn responds to indicators of season and environment. We could say that the bird's instincts plan backward from the ideal time for birth. A chick will do best if it is born early in a stretch of mild weather when food is plen-

Brood Parasitism

Propagation is no picnic. Defending a territory, charming a mate, building a nest, incubating eggs, feeding babies minute after minute—it's a lot of work to raise a family of birds.

Some birds have found a way to satisfy the biological drive to reproduce, without all the muss and fuss. They simply lay their eggs in the nest of a pair of birds from another species, and leave them to the care of their hosts. This is called brood parasitism.

Birds from five families sponsor foster children this way. Perhaps the most considerate is South America's black-headed duck, which is the only precocial brood parasite. The female lays an egg in a host nest, but doesn't remove or destroy any of the other eggs in the nest, as do most parasitic mothers. Once the young duck hatches, it does not accept food from the foster parents (as do all others); and at the age of two days, it checks out of the host's hotel, taking nothing away except perhaps the mystery of its presence.

The altricial brood parasites are not such perfect guests. Most damage the family configuration of their hosts in one way or another—once the female parasite has snuck in and laid her egg (usually very quickly: cowbirds and cuckoos take about five seconds for the job) nothing is ever quite the same. Some hosts will abandon a nest that contains a strange egg, even if it also contains a clutch of their own. Some will simply build a new platform nest on top of the old, letting all of the eggs in it spoil. In one perverse case, a researcher took three eggs from a garden warbler's nest, and put in three lesser whitethroat eggs. When the warbler laid her fourth natural egg the next day, she looked at the eggs around it, decided something was wrong, and —in accordance with a bird's instinct to remove foreign objects from the nest— promptly tipped her own "odd" egg over the side!

Robins, catbirds, and a few others seem to be pretty good at detecting the eggs of interlopers and destroying them. Most hosts are either less sharp, or less persnickety— they simply accept the strange egg and incubate it with their own. Some of the parasitic cowbirds have a concern about the foster parents' sense of clutch size: the female who sneaks in and lays an egg in a host nest will then remove and eat one of the host's eggs. She will do this until she has spread around a clutch of her own six eggs, one to a nest; she will lay 2 to 4 clutches a season. Cowbirds are the champions of easygoing parasitism—they barge in, without being picky, on about 250 species, and will lay in nests that already have several other cowbird eggs in them.

The European cuckoo is subtle in the art of intruding her eggs into another bird's nest. She has a wizard-like ability to produce eggs that imitate the form of her host's eggs—in size, shape, and coloration. Cuckoos usually parasitize smaller birds, so most of them lay much smaller eggs than would be expected of such a relatively large songbird; but if the host is a larger bird, the cuckoo somehow comes up with a *bigger* egg than it should. Whole "races" of cuckoos have evolved to take advantage of resident

The cuckoo chick hatches a day ahead of its nestmates (bunnocks, in this case), and—despite its blindness—launches a fatal attack on them, rolling their eggs onto its shoulders and pushing them over the edge of the nest.

populations of hosts in certain regions, and their eggs reflect the specialization they have accepted. Finnish cuckoos lay blue eggs, to fit in with the redstarts they impose themselves on there; Hungarian cuckoos opt for light green eggs splotched with dark brown to match those of the great reed warblers who accommodate them in that country.

Once the cuckoo's egg has been accepted, the trouble for the host's family has only begun. A cuckoo observes the construction of her host's nest and lays her egg coeval with the host's clutch. However, the cuckoo needs only 12 days of incubation, so it hatches 1 to 2 days ahead of its nestmates. After only a few hours, the cuckoo chick shows that it was born with more strength—and a great deal more initiative—than most altricial young, when, despite its nakedness and blindness, it bumps its way around the nest and begins to eject its unborn competitors. Its method is fantastic: if it encounters an egg with its back, it spreads its wings to make a hollow for the egg and backs like Sisyphus in reverse up the incline of the nest's wall to the edge, where it rolls its foster brother or sister into the void. It wastes no time in its industrious murder; it seems to know it is working against a clock, and it will clean out a nest in no time. The parents—mystified, no doubt, but still driven by instinct—feed the strapping cuckoo youth by default. In Europe, the sight of a delicate little adult warbler hopelessly feeding a spanking huge cuckoo more than twice its size, crammed into the tiny nest like too much chocolate ice cream on a dainty cone, provides a common look at one of nature's wildest oxymorons.

(continued)

*No, the wood thrush didn't change its taste
in color three-fourths of the way through
this clutch; the white speckled egg belongs
to a cowbird. These parasites don't bother
with the egg mimicry mastered by cuckoos,
but their plainly foreign eggs are most
often accepted by the hosts.*

Equally murderous is the hatchling of several species of the African honey guide. This intruder is born with a tool to eliminate its competition, not in the egg phase, but *mano a mano*. The honey guide's upper and lower mandibles possess dagger-like pincers that give it a piercing, killing grip, which it uses on its host's rightful heirs, one by one, until it alone remains to claim the fortune of food and comfort.

Cowbirds, the most numerous intruders, are far more polite, except for the single egg theft mentioned above. They do not disguise their eggs, they do not eject the competition, and they seem to have a keener sense that, by wiping out the future of host species, they are wiping out their own potential abodes. No one is certain why brood parasitism evolved—some say it was probably a convenience that became a habit, then a habit that became an instinct. In the case of cowbirds, a charming theory suggests that they, as their name indicates, have a close relationship with large animals of the range, following as the stock stomp through the grass raising clouds of insects. Long ago their main partners were probably the great, ceaselessly moving herds of bison. The cowbirds, to keep eating, had to keep moving with the nomads of the plains. Even when their mating season was at hand, they could not pause for the amenities of courtship, territory, nesting. They laid their eggs where they could, and moved on, following their destiny. They have fared much better than the bison.

tiful. These two conditions usually coincide: the most common food for nestlings is insects and worms, which are most plentiful in the warm seasons of spring and summer. Fruit and berries ripen in summer and fall, for fledglings graduating from their protein-rich baby diet and starting to find their own food; for raptors, the summer is a crowded time, with lots of animals abroad in sky and field, populations ready to be thinned of the slow and careless.

In some parts of the world the season of plenty comes abruptly and lasts but a short time, so eggs must be laid and sometimes even hatched in winter. Antarctic penguins hatch in −90° weather, but a brief summer soon arrives; the chicks gorge and grow fat just in time for the next dark winter. Not only longitude is important; elevation plays its part in the schedule of laying. Birds of the same species in valley, hill, or mountain environments lay at different times according to their level; higher birds will lay eggs considerably later than the birds lower down.

The act of laying the egg is generally arduous; a female spreads her wings a bit, leans forward, pants, squeezes backward, and ejects the egg. Once she has begun laying, she follows a pattern for the accretion of her family. Some birds lay only one egg, but most produce more (especially the passerines). Usually the ovary does not release an ovum to begin its path down the oviduct until the previous egg is out, so the time required for the formation of the whole egg is essentially the interval between layings. In most passerines, woodpeckers, and small shorebirds this is about 24 hours. The majority of the remaining species separate their eggs by 36 to 48 hours. Some of the larger birds take four or five days; so does the kiwi, who labors over the world's largest egg relative to body size: its weight is 25 percent of the female adult who lays it.

The size of the clutch is fairly constant in each species. General limits are imposed by nest size, egg size, and the parents' ability to feed nestlings. However, there are varying patterns that seem to be related to specific conditions of the

environment or the particular bird. Generally, birds subject to harsher conditions or greater peril lay more eggs: northern birds lay more than their southern kin, birds in areas with more predators lay more than those in safer spots. If you are a bird interested in pushing your species into the future, you throw more babies into the more dangerous environments, hoping that enough survive to carry on.

Clutch size may increase during bumper-crop years, when conditions produce more light and better food. The traditional size of a species' clutch may steadily evolve, too, if there is a constant increase in food supply: several Australian eagle species responded to the introduction of rabbits in their land by laying more eggs each year and rearing more eaglets. If the environment will support more new birds, the parents sense it—and they lay the eggs. The increase is not wild, however; adults seem to know that there are a lot of others doing the same thing, and that this year's babies are next year's competitors. So the numbers go up incrementally.

Some birds lay a fixed number of eggs regardless of what happens to the clutch's size; if an egg is broken or stolen, the female does not replace it with a new one. If an egg is added to the nest, she does not cut her productivity to count it. These are called *determinate* layers: they have an absolute sense of the clutch's size. *Indeterminate* layers, on the other hand, have a relative sense of the clutch—if eggs are removed the female lays until she has the count up to the right number, and if eggs are added she stops laying.

Any poultry farmer knows this: removing the morning's eggs keeps the hen a'laying. I discovered it with a canary, who surprised me one day by laying a lovely but doomed (unfertilized) egg in her food tray. I removed it, thinking to save her the anguish of a fruitless incubation. She lay another. I removed it. She kept laying, and I, with the stubborn goodwill of the ignoramus, kept yanking them out, discreetly, during her exercise flights. Finally, after 12 eggs in 12 days, she gave up. (The next year, thinking that such productivity deserves fruition, I set her up with a mate.)

My overextension of the canary was nothing to feel bad about. Fifty years ago, a researcher spent a spring swiping the eggs of a yellow-shafted flicker, and the female spent the spring replacing them: in 73 days she laid 72 eggs (the normal flicker clutch has 6 to 8). Other experiments have driven many different indeterminate layers to similar ovulatory frenzies.

Another distinction in the behavior surrounding eggs involves the start of incubation. Some birds begin incubating after the first egg is laid, while others wait for the entire clutch. The different results are obvious. In the first case, the hatching of young is staggered, and a brood is a hierarchy of older and younger brothers and sisters. When all eggs are incubated as a unit, the young hatch more or less simultaneously.

Incubating from the start protects the whole clutch, but having chicks of staggered ages can cause problems in the rearing of a brood—disjointed feeding demands, competition among siblings, even fratricide. In some cases, parents treat later eggs with disdain, and sometimes they even join in the abuse of the youngest hatchling. There is no unluckier thing to be in nature than the runt of a lammergeier brood; the parents usually shred their second child (the clutch contains only two eggs). It could be that these large, rather aggressive vultures haven't yet coordi-

Incubation—the peace before the pandemonium of parenthood. (trumpeter swan)

nated their laying instincts with their fear of food shortage; or it could be that this killing comes from obsolete instincts the ancient causes of which are now merely symbolic.

Most birds of prey incubate from the first egg; so do many water birds (loons, grebes, gulls), along with swifts, hornbills, hummingbirds, and parrots. Most passerines wait until the full clutch is assembled, as do ducks. This gives the parents a sudden, huge challenge—to feed a family of five or six many times a day—but it also lets them define their roles absolutely. For a couple of weeks they are incubators; then for a few weeks they are slaves. Perhaps these birds perform best when absorbed in clearly delineated tasks and are weak at improvising priorities when many different demands are made on them simultaneously.

We clever humans may see no special challenge in the bird's task of assessing the completeness of its clutch—but it is very unlikely that birds count, or remember how many eggs they laid the year before. Scientists have generally settled on the theory that egg-laying is controlled by the pressure of the eggs against the belly of the female—when it "feels right" the hormones that keep her oviduct cranking shut down.

This intelligent-abdomen-theory is probably not as strange as it sounds. Incubation—warming eggs, rather then simply sheltering them—is a sensitive and active process, and most birds definitely do it with their bellies, or, more specifically, with a part of the belly called a brood patch.

Brood patches are spots of bare skin through which heat can pass by relatively direct conduction to the eggshell. Birds develop them just before they are called on to incubate, thanks once again to hormones. Down feathers—which keep body heat from spreading—fall out (or, in the case of ducks, are plucked) in a certain small area. The exposed skin then grows soft and effulgent with blood vessels. Though the patches seem to be initiated by a female sex hormone, they develop on both parents in most families with shared incubation. The patches are very

effective; studies have estimated that they make as much as a +12° difference in the heat provided by the sitting parent.

Twelve degrees could certainly be the margin of life for the embryo in the egg. In general, birds need to keep their eggs at a constant temperature of around 95 to 102°, about ten degrees below their own body temperature. An initial warming-up brings them to the right heat, and also brings the brood patch into full function—stabilizing its special circulatory and dermic features. From that point on, the egg must be kept at the right temperature.

This means a lot more than simply sitting on the egg around the clock for 12 to 90 days. For one thing, temperature is not regulated simply by being *increased*. The eggs of a tern on the beach or a nighthawk on a rooftop can get too hot as easily as a penguin egg can get too cool. The incubating parent may stand over the eggs with wings spread, letting the air reach the eggs but shading them from sunlight. In several species of ground-nesting shorebirds—skimmers and plovers—the parent about to relieve its mate on the nest will prepare for incubatory duty by dipping its belly into shallow water, lowering its abdominal temperature, and soaking up moisture that will be spread to the eggs. Although this definitely improves the eggs' cooling, its more direct effect may be to keep the parent's temperature down—which is in turn passed on to the eggs. Parents in the sun often pant as they sit for the same reason.

Sometimes the incubating parent must leave the nest to forage for food. Often the bird will pull some leaves or feathers over the eggs, but many eggs have a protection of their own: the shell coloration in several species—brownish marks in ground nesters, bright blue in tree nesters—is designed to repel rays of the near-infrared part of the solar spectrum.

In nests with more than 2 to 3 eggs, the temperature varies a lot between the center egg (directly against the brood patch) and the egg on the margin of the nest (nearly against the ground or the air). To keep the heat evenly distributed, the parent uses its bill to rotate the eggs

A male wandering albatross rotates his egg in the nest to prevent adhesions between interior membranes and the inner surface of the shell.

more or less in sequence, so that everyone gets a turn in the center, on the fringe, snug against the belly, and down near the bottom.

This turning of the eggs serves several purposes not only within the nest, but within the egg itself. Just as there is a stratification of heat in the configuration of eggs, there is a great difference between the temperature at the top of an egg (the part nearest the parent) and the temperature at its bottom—sometimes as much as 20°! In turning the eggs over as well as changing their nest position, the parent is keeping all parts warm. Whether a bird does this a lot (7 to 8 times an hour for some passerines) or a little (once an hour for the pheasants) may be as much

a matter of personality or habit as of need. But then, we cannot assess all of the needs, because we don't know all of the things turning might do for the egg. We do know that it keeps the embryo's membranes from adhering to the interior surface of the shell; eggs that are not turned not only hatch less frequently, but often produce deformed chicks, indicating that the embryo and its fluids need to be relatively free within the shell to rest in the appropriate position.

There are few things that seem as magically secret as the development of an embryo within an egg. How does something that starts as a bunch of liquids come out with a beak and scaly feet and feathers? Actually, only one of the "liquids" becomes the bird: the yolk contains the fertilized ovum and the material that will nourish its growth and supply the fundamental tissue. What we call the white of the egg supplies amino acids and minerals. It also serves as a protective fluid, and keeps the embryo-*cum*-yolk from drying out during the tremendous changes that begin taking place after incubation begins.

Within the germinal "seed" of the embryo, the blastoderm, a fabulously diverse multiplication of cells begins. Soon after the egg is laid the cells form three layers. The outermost is the ectoderm, which will produce the skin, nervous system, and brain; the middle layer is the mesoderm, producing cartilage, bones, muscles, heart, kidneys, and other organs; innermost is the endoderm, from which the lungs, stomach, and liver arise. The ectoderm begins to form a tube that will become the spinal column of the bird. The first part of this structure elaborates itself into a bulb that will become the brain. Other organs begin to form rapidly, and within a few days the embryo looks much like a young human fetus—that is, rather like a tadpole. But not for long. By the time the incubation has reached its halfway point (only a week or so in many species), the reptilian embryo has a beak, feather tracts, incipient wings, feet, and tail. Before long it is a baby bird about to outgrow its snug casing.

From the beginning the whole organism is supported by a strong system of blood vessels that bring the embryo rich proteins and fats from the yolk and oxygen infused through the porous shell. Wastes are processed in a sac called the allantois, which is an exterior ballooning of the gut. The finite space of the egg's interior contains a shifting balance of exterior substances and temporary organs, the purpose of which is to support interior conversions of those substances into organs that will take over these functions. There is literally no room for error—no retardation in one bud of development, no overproduction in another.

When the egg was laid the blastoderm was a tiny spot surrounded by food and water, but by the time of hatching the embryo has consumed almost everything around it. The allantois has dried up as the kidneys came to life; the albumen (which was mostly water) has been absorbed; the yolk has been consumed through the umbilicus, most of it gradually, but with a big gulp saved for the chick to take in just before hatching. This is a push of nourishment that will see the hatchling through the transition from shell-bred to well-fed—one to grow on, so to speak.

Chances are, the young bird will need a boost just for the hatching. The shell of an egg is thinner at the end of the incubation period because the embryo has absorbed lime from it during the formation of its bones, but it is still a tough barrier to break from a cramped position—especially when such a contorted athletic feat is the creature's first locomotive act. The embryo is equipped with two tools for the task: a sharp protrusion from the end of its bill (the "egg tooth"), and a special muscle in the back of the neck. These will give more punch to its poke.

The fully developed embryo goes through a kind of prelude to hatching a couple of days before it actually attacks the shell. As a warm-up for breaching the lime, the bird jabs the tip of its beak through the membrane at the rounder end of the shell, pushing into the airspace that was formed in the earliest stages of the egg. This is where the bird takes its first breath, a quick nip of terribly stale air, but nevertheless a huge step toward the outdoors. The chick will breathe in this space, but because the exchange of carbon dioxide and oxygen through the shell is so poor, its main oxygen source will still be the array of vessels on the surface of the allantois. Many chicks begin to peep during this time, too.

A day or two later, the chick will begin in earnest to push its bill at the shell, using all of its purchase inside the oval to power its thrusts. The bill finally cracks the perfect surface, and the chick, as if assured now of eventual triumph, cools its frantic haste a bit and adopts a technique. (Anyone who has forgotten a can opener on a camping trip and opened a can of beans

with a Phillips screwdriver knows the trick: you poke a circle of holes in the lid, then you poke through the strips of metal that remain between the holes. Eventually a circular piece falls out, and there you are.)

This is what the chick does: it cuts a pretty neat line around the circumference of the shell's blunt end. If necessary, it then pokes through strips of shell and membrane between its holes. As soon as it senses the necessary weakness in the lid's adherence to the main shell, it tucks its beak, jams its head against the lid, and pushes. As the lid detaches, the chick hikes its legs up and works a toe or two over the edge of the shell's main body, like a kid climbing a fence; and soon, with this added force, it propels itself onto the floor of its nest. There it will lie, panting and spent, for a matter of minutes or hours, until the parents feed it or lead it off to find food of its own.

The job of hatching takes as little as a couple of hours in some birds (pheasants are perhaps the quickest, sometimes going from first crack to emergence in less than an hour), and as much as a few days in others (two days for the European wren, four for some shearwaters).

There are two distinct kinds of chicks: altricial (helpless, blind, featherless) and precocial (mobile, wide-eyed, feathered). The difference begins in the egg: in general, the eggs of the species born with greater readiness for the world have larger yolks (35 percent of egg volume) and longer incubation times (17 to 37 days) than those of the less mature hatchlings (20 percent and 11 to 19 days). The period of "total" development from egg-laying to independent adolescence may be similar in duration between roughly similar species, though one is precocial and the other altricial; the difference is that one develops in the egg and the other in the nest. Logically, the species with exposed nests tend to produce precocial young (also called nidifugous, or nest-leaving), while those ensconced in better-protected shelters bear altricial chicks (nidicolous, or nest-dwelling).

Precocial chicks emerge and let their feathers dry; after a few hours, most of them are ready to be led to food they will eat themselves. They walk or swim; the parents simply lead the way and point out what should be eaten. Independence notwithstanding, the bond with parents is very strong, and most precocial chicks "live at home" for the 3 to 12 weeks from when they hatch to when they fly off. This is a time of rather slow physical development, compared to the altricial young; we might say the precocious birds have longer childhoods of greater skill. These species—mostly ground or water feeders good at walking, running, or swimming, including most water birds, shorebirds, and gallinaceous birds

A pheasant chick hatches, dries in the sun, and will be on its feet by the time its nestmate is out.

—have evolved by trading protection for capability. Their young spend a long time at a fairly vulnerable stage, instead of a shorter time at an utterly helpless stage.

At first glance, the altricial young seem to be pitifully retarded in comparison with precocial chicks. They are more like bleached salamanders than birds—nude and shivering, with bruise-colored knobs where alert eyes should be, and ridiculous nubby wings that look like forelimbs from which the useful part has been amputated. We may be tempted to think that with a little more yolk and a little more patience, these species—hawks, owls, pelicans, parrots, pigeons, kingfishers, woodpeckers, swifts, hummingbirds, and passerines—*could* have had a snappy item with bright eyes and dancing feet, like the plover or duck. Perhaps they just need to evolve.

Despite appearances, this altricial brown pelican chick is perfectly healthy; in fact, in a couple of weeks it will be ahead of these precocial avocets, though they seem to have a head start. Note that all unhatched eggs in these nests have been pipped—the hatchlings are on their way, all emerging together.

Alternatives to the Belly

The soft, expansive flesh of the abdomen, settled snugly down over the securely nested eggs, seems the perfect incubator. There's just something about *bellies*—perhaps because they loom so large in human fertility, we certainly see them as a natural surface for the bodily nurture of eggs.

But some birds look down at their *feet*—their dry, scaly, webbed feet—and think, Ah, just the thing to warm my eggs, whereupon they step upon the fragile things and commence to incubate, more or less upright. These are birds of the gannet family, including the boobies. They are tropical seabirds, very well adapted for life on the water. They plunge and dive as well as any birds in the world and are capable of spending long periods far away from land, though they return to breed. Some of them nest on cliffs, some on the ground; most are colonial, and all build only rudimentary structures for their eggs (usually only one or two).

One of their adaptations for aquatic performance is a flamboyantly webbed foot, with webbing between all four well-spread toes (rather than between three, as is normal in ducks, geese, swans, gulls, terns). The feet of the gannets and boobies are fabulous flapping things; one cannot see them without imagining the *smap smap smap* they would make on a rock when they were fresh out of the ocean.

It so happens that the skin between the toes is extremely thin, and well endowed with blood vessels. These two qualities mean that warmth from the blood could pass quickly through the skin. This serves the birds well as a cooling mechanism—they lose heat effectively through the feet, the way a desert fox or hare sheds it through veiny ears. Sometimes the birds even wet their feet with defecation to hasten the cooling.

The warmth that passes through the skin need not be thrown away, however; when warmth is needed, it can be directly conducted to whatever the gannet can wrap its cellophane webs around. This means eggs, the only objects in a tropical environment that need to gain heat rather than lose it. So instead of hunkering belly-down over the eggs hour after hour—which might cause the parent to overheat—the bird stands and delivers.

Booby eggs on a sun-baked beach require less additional heat in incubation than the eggs of another bird who uses its feet. The female emperor penguin lays her single egg on the ice of Antarctica and hies off to the water to eat for 8 to 10 weeks. The air temperature is about −35°. The nestless egg would freeze in a matter of minutes if the father weren't there to step in and care for it. But what to do? Penguins are notoriously vertical; their feet are not placed amidships as in most birds that can swing their bodies horizontally over their eggs and lower the belly with just the right degree of pressure. The penguin's feet are placed more like ours, but with much

With feet like these, who needs to nestle?

shorter legs—as if our feet came at the midpoint of our thighs—and thus the only way the bird could use the underside of its belly would be to lie with its full weight on the eggs, with crunching results.

Appropriately enough, the male emperor figured out a way to turn the troublesome placement of his feet into an incubatory solution: he rolls the egg up onto the top of his feet and droops a fatty fold of his belly skin over the egg like a makeshift pouch. Thus he is still able to stand in a natural terrestrial position while removing the egg from the ice and air and warming it with the heat of his lower abdomen and fleshy feet.

The only thing the male emperor penguin cannot do while he incubates is move. That this also prevents him from eating is apparently no problem: the stoic father fasts until the weather has warmed and the slow embryo is ready to hatch, at which point the female usually returns to feed and brood the chick. If she is delayed, the father feeds the baby a protein-rich secretion from his esophagus. During his fast, which can last 115 days, the male loses up to 45 percent of his body weight. When his mate relieves him, he wobbles toward the sea, there to take his turn at weeks of eating, building up fat for the winter that will soon come.

Short-eared owls, unlike the avocets on page 133, hatch in a series—usually one per day. This makes for a brood of chicks with different ages, as can be seen in this quintet. The runt of the brood starts out several days behind its brethren; it may never catch up, either starving or being killed.

Actually, the species with altricial young are more highly evolved than their precocial brethren. At the age of two days, this would seem hard to believe; but then an astonishing process of development begins, and the blind salamanders are transformed into strapping, fully feathered young adults who easily outstrip the erstwhile prodigies. After two weeks, while the plover is still a snappy chick weeks away from leaving the nest, the young Baltimore oriole is out on its own, flying well and finding its own worms.

There is nothing in the rest of the animal world like this period of dazzling maturation; we could be forgiven for thinking it a metamorphosis rather than a sequential development. Essentially, the chick requires only one thing—food, and a lot of it—to release its storm of cells and systems. It is born capable of nothing but eating; its brain and senses make up about half the percentage of body weight that these organs do in a precocial chick, while its intestinal tract's share is twice that of the nidifuge. But once it is given its food, the nestbound chick's metabolism converts it into new growth, the sophistication of which is matched by its sheer mass. In three weeks a cuckoo multiplies its weight by a factor of 50—going from 2 gm to 100—and acquires in the process a nervous system more sophisticated than that of a precocial chick of the same age.

The feeding of the altricial young thus gets almost all of the parents' attention. It is a one-dimensional demand and most of the tiny bird's features are oriented toward communicating it unequivocally. Chicks have colored beaks that they open in wide gapes and stretch toward the parent with food, making a brightly outlined receptacle. Inside their mouths, the chicks of many species flash even more bright markings, literally targets for the parents to aim at. (One of the most wonderful "improvisations" of the parasitic European cuckoo is its ability to develop inner-mouth marks similar to those of the chicks it is joining or replacing in a host nest.)

Though the brilliant beaks and interior growths serve as targets, and are especially useful in species with enclosed nests (where parents must feed in the dark), their main use may be to stimulate the feeding instinct in adult birds. Along with particular cries from the chicks, the sight of displayed hunger drives parents immediately to find food and cram it into the right cavity. The feeding is usually beak-to-beak. Some adult birds bring back insects or worms and parcel them out directly to the straining nestlings; some swallow the food as they find it in the field and regurgitate it into the mouths of the young. Hummingbirds do this with their nectar, going farther than most: they stick their long beaks almost into the stomachs of the chicks. Conversely, pelicans simply open their maw and let their young stumble up and dip deeply into the crop full of food.

Feeding by regurgitation allows the parents to hunt more efficiently: they can take in a great deal of food that could not be easily carried back to the nest in discrete units. Most young are fed high-protein animal foods—insects, worms, fish—at first, no matter what the adult diet will be (house sparrows are 95 percent vegetarian, but feed their young a diet that is 70 percent animal). The hunting parent who tries to catch another moth while holding one in its beak will

probably lose both. Using the crop or stomach like a fisherman's creel is a far more efficient means of collection. It also has the advantage of presenting food to the very young chicks with a coating of digestive juices from the adult; sometimes the chicks need a little help breaking down their food, until their enzymes and acids kick in fully.

Some adult birds who range far away from the nest, and thus hunt for longer periods, go ahead and begin digesting the food they collect. Upon returning to the nest they regurgitate to their young a mush that is easy to swallow and digest. As the young develop, the mush contains more solid matter.

Pigeons, doves, and flamingos feed their young a liquid, too, but it is not made up of partially digested grubs or fish. These birds actually produce a kind of "crop milk" (creamy white in pigeons and doves, bright red in flamingos) made of epithelial tissues from the crop, similar to the milk of some mammals in its composition. Birds have no mammary glands, but in these cases the crop's means of production is not unlike the process that creates true milk.

Most raptors go to the other extreme, challenging their developing young with food items that are increasingly difficult to ingest. At first, a hawk will bring its snake or mouse to the nest and tear it into bites for the chicks. But very soon, the baby will simply be presented with dead prey, relatively intact. Instinctively, the chick will fall upon it with gusto if not expertise, using its already sharp beak and talons to cut its own meat.

In some species whose instincts do not inspire such spontaneous butchery, the female takes responsibility for preparing food for the consumption of the babies, while the male is left simply to gather it. If the female dies while the chicks are very young, the male may not take over her task—he will bring whole animals to the nest and watch idiotically as his offspring starve.

However, in most adult birds the feeding instinct includes a sense of how to deliver the

A pelican invites its chick to fish for itself in the parent's catch, stored inside the crop and bill.

Flamingos make "milk" for their chicks and feed them beak-to-beak.

Green heron chicks strike a gawky you-can't-see-me pose similar to that of the bittern.

goods. Though the parents need occasional stimulation from the chicks, once they begin they are absolutely compelled. Experiments and field observations have shown with many species that parents deprived of their chicks will still bring food to the nest. In some cases, they will even stuff the food into any handy receptacle that gives them the feeling of release: cracks in a wall, knots in a tree, offspring of other birds. In perhaps the oddest case of misplaced feeding instinct, a North Carolina cardinal regularly fed worms to goldfish that swam to the edge of a man-made pool and gaped like the babies the bird must have lost.

The adult bird probably requires every bit of compulsion its instincts can muster, for feeding altricial young is a stupendous task. Some passerines make as many as 1,000 trips to the nest in a single day, usually taking a small tidbit at a time. The great tit will feed its young 60 times an hour, about 900 times a day; the house wren, 500; the nuthatch, 350. These are all small insect eaters who do not regurgitate. Larger birds tend to bring back larger meals, especially the raptors. Golden eagles will feed their eaglets a rabbit or the equivalent a couple of times a day.

Though feeding is the primary focus of both chick and adult, there are other duties the parents must meet if the fantastic growth of the altricial young is to reach its rapid fruition. The chicks still need to be kept within a certain range of temperature; outside the egg as in, they are unable for a while to regulate their own body heat. The parents "brood" for weeks—snuggling the birds and sharing warmth within the insulation of the nest. (Precocial young require brooding as much as altricial.) In many cases, as with eggs, the chicks must be sheltered from the sun with coverings of feathers, leaves, or a canopy of wings. Adult herons may be driven by extreme heat to spray their offspring with defecation, the evaporation of which cools the chicks and keeps them alive, albeit dirty.

As a rule, young birds handle cold much better than heat, sometimes slipping into a torpid state—a kind of impromptu hibernation, almost like a reptile—to survive a stretch of chill and/ or hunger. Hunger and chill often come together if the weather is wet. Insects don't fly as plentifully in the rain, so insectivores may have to take longer trips away from the nest, exposing the young to wetness; it's a trade-off different species handle in different ways. Some will sit on the young in the nest through the rain, preferring the chances of surviving starvation to hypothermia. Others will look for food and let the young weather it out.

Chicks need protection from predators as well as from rain and extreme temperature. As mentioned earlier, the first line of defense is camouflage, at which most birds are fairly good. Some nestlings, such as bitterns, are born with the instincts to perform their species' hiding behavior (sticking the neck in the air to imitate the pattern of reeds in the bittern's case). In many others, an adult who cannot hide the chicks will utter an alarm cry, to which the chicks respond by hunkering down and freezing on the spot.

A trumpeter swan's defensive posture frightens the yellow-headed blackbird, which strayed too close to the swan's nest.

This common merganser chick can swim—but why not take a free ride?

The predator may pass by, leaving them unharmed.

If it does not, there are a few options left. Some adults pick up their chicks and flee, sometimes holding them in a peculiar grasp. The American finfoot has scoops of skin beneath the wings to hold its young as it swims or flies away from trouble. A sandpiper, willet, or woodcock will squeeze its chick between its adult legs and fly. Raptors grasp the chicks in their talons, rails in their beaks; several water birds swim away with young on their backs.

Such fleeing is unwieldy and slow. If the predator is too close and too quick, the parent on the nest may try the ruse of pretending to be injured, seeming to offer itself as easy prey as it limps away from the nest, dragging an apparently broken wing. Adults never truly offer themselves in place of their children, but in this ploy the predator doesn't know that. It may follow the "injured" bird—usually making a commotion to draw attention away from the nest—until the adult deems its nest is out of sight and mind, at which time it springs back to full speed and hides itself.

As a last resort, the defending adults may attack the predator, hissing at it, striking it with the beak or feet, vomiting or defecating on it in swooping flight, or, in the case of the fulmars, squirting foul-smelling oil at the predator. In colonial nesting grounds, a predator may find itself surrounded by a civil defense initiative—

Herding the flock. (Canada geese)

but not always. A marabou may waltz in among flamingos and pick chicks off nests as idle parents watch, befuddled; the same may happen in clusters of penguins.

Many birds seem handcuffed when their eggs are attacked, but will fight to defend a chick. This is probably because the propagatory investment increases as the offspring grows—from egg to hatchling to nearly fledged youngster—and the parent's instinct is to fight with greater zeal for the offspring that is closest to carrying on the species. A three-day-old egg doesn't represent a tremendous expenditure of effort, nor does it satisfy fully one's urge to reproduce; so when a gull or black snake comes and threatens to eat it, the adult is not often willing to risk its life. It can, after all, lay another egg pretty easily. But a three-week-old chick, fat and feathered and ready to fly in a day or two, is a precious product representing a fantastic outlay of work and resources, and it *looks* just like the parent who is compelled to replicate itself. So the same snake will get a fight this time.

If the parents of altricial young keep the predators away, the food coming, and the temperature right, there remains one last duty that in its way is a measure of their success: keeping the nest clean. A young bird who eats a lot defecates a lot. The longer it stays alive, the more its feces will stack up. Nests, however, must remain snug and dry, to preserve their insulating qualities, and most adult birds instinctively jettison any

The pose of defiance comes early in a bird's instincts: a red-tailed hawk nestling defends its sibling.

foreign objects. Eggshells are usually removed soon after chicks hatch, and inedible parts of food items are taken away and discarded after meals. Some birds even chuck banded babies out of the nest in an effort to remove the bright aluminum band a human has placed on one leg of the chick for purposes of monitoring populations.

For some birds, sanitation is no problem—precocial young defecate outside the nest, and many raptor chicks hike themselves over the edge of their aeries to eject their fumets. But nestbound altricial chicks—especially passerines—must go where they will, as it were.

Removing feces would be a terrible task were it not for a special adaptation that passerines have evolved: the chicks excrete their wastes in tough mucous sacs that serve the same function as twist-tied plastic trash bags. The parents pick them up and get rid of them, very neatly. In many species the adults swallow them in the early days (perhaps because the excrement contains undigested food and therefore holds nutrition that cannot be wasted), and later drop them, either beneath the nest or in flight. The disposal is pretty casual in most birds, but swallows and martins make a special effort to drop their sacs in water, and the female lyrebird immerses them in water or buries them.

In the loosely built nests of some non-passerines, the feces—unbagged—fall through the cracks, well out of the bowl of occupation. And herons, just as they sometimes use their own excrement to cool off their chicks, may use that of the chicks to cool their large, twiggy nests. The liquid feces drop and evaporate just beneath the occupied area, lowering the temperature in the nest.

And so the childhood of the bird passes—of

the lucky bird, that is, the one whose egg did not break or succumb to cold, whose parents or siblings did not eat it, who did not freeze in a spring storm or bake in a summer heat wave, who was well-fed by parents able to locate thousands of suitable meals, who was sheltered from the falcons and gulls, monkeys, foxes, and snakes, whose nest was clean and adequately roomy, and, finally, who was able one day to leap into space and, at the peril of a killing fall, fly away.

Behavior during the transition from the nest to the world varies from species to species. Sometimes it is a curiously quick and unceremonious thing: the swift's fledglings simply leave while the parents are away from the nest. Sometimes the departure is carefully supervised. Young murres are encouraged by a series of parental entreaty calls to fly down at dusk from their nestless ledges even before their primary flight feathers have developed, and then to swim. To protect the chicks from gulls during their awkward, coasting descent to the water, parents may fly just above them, interposing themselves between prey and would-be predator. Most species with altricial chicks spend a couple of days breaking them in to their new independence, especially as the whole brood may not be ready to leave on the same day. In such cases, one parent will move

Most birds are banded on the foot (see the hornbill on page 77). But these collars allow researchers to record a goose's identifying number through binoculars, saving it the trauma of being caught and handled—if not the trauma of looking very strange to its flock.

Cattle egrets over Kenya.

afield with the fledglings, encouraging their experiments with flight and foraging (usually by refusing to feed them), while the other adult remains to care for the nestlings.

Albatross, petrel, and shearwater parents are as unsentimental as swift fledglings. They feed their young on a schedule that takes into account the imminent time of departure, fattening them up to the point that the "chicks" are heavier than the parents. Then, a few days before the young should fledge, the parents disappear. The fat kids are left to survive on their reserves, burning off the excess weight and taking shape as independent adults until, finally, they are trim and hungry. Then they leave on their own.

Whether the young whisk themselves away, or are coaxed into departure, they leave the nest and their parents without much ado, fully capable in a remarkably short time of finding their own food, fleeing from danger, and, as the season draws to an end, of performing the most astounding feat of physical and mental determination in the world of nature. Come fall, they join the birds around them, of all generations, and they migrate.

Migration, Apotheosis of Flight

In the thriving days of early fall, those of us who notice birds feel happily surrounded by the richness of avian life. Looking out at the grosbeaks, finches, sparrows, and jays on our feeders, we realize that we see more birds these days than people. We recognize many of them, too—there's a pair of mockingbirds whose nest, built on the top of our garden fence, we were able to assess in every phase of its construction, and whose offspring we watched grow from pink newts to cocky-tailed adolescents; in fact, we spot two of the new birds on the branches of that tulip poplar over there.

It is a fine, noisy, fluttery world we live in. We go away for a weekend, making sure that our feeders are full; during our trip we miss the company of the familiar birds and look forward to their chatter and dashing about when we return.

But on our first morning back, they do not show up. We wait by the window, drinking more than the usual number of cups of coffee as an excuse to linger. No action out there. We overfill the feeders. Only a few chickadees drop by. There are occasional distant groups of birds in the sky, but our friends seem to have left us.

There is no absence in the world like the sudden subtraction of bird life from an environment. One week the songbirds are all over the place; the next week they are gone. It is easy to feel bereft and betrayed, especially when someone tells us, with scientific detachment, that the warblers we nurtured through their precarious breeding season are now cracking sesame seeds on somebody else's bird feeder in balmy Brazil.

There are no real foreigners in the world of birds, and no homebodies either. The unsurpassed mobility that allows birds to find food and build nests wherever their instincts lead them has its apotheosis twice a year when the birds are compelled to show that the world is their home—by migrating.

Migration is the regular movement from one place of living to another. It is different from aimless roaming or patterned hunting: when you migrate you pick up and move, on a schedule. Most birds migrate and very few of them do so by slipping into the suburbs of their breeding grounds—they travel over oceans, cities, deserts, seas of ice, top-secret nuclear weapon-testing ranges, highways, elite estates, tundra, pampas, slums, canyons. Probably the birds flying directly over the playing field of the World Series every fall outnumber the people watching the games on television! Migrating birds often fly unseen, high in the night. We have no idea where they have gone. We can only wait, until spring, to see if they come back.

Migration is one of the unsolvable mysteries of bird life. A bird weighing a couple of ounces will up and fly thousands of miles across perilous territory that offers no place to alight or eat, losing a quarter of its body weight, risking exhaustion that would drop it into the ocean like rain, only to arrive in a place which, if it doesn't offer immediate nourishment and shelter, will become its grave. It seems like such a foolish undertaking.

(continued)

But it must not be. Evolution does not favor fools. Migration works for birds—not for every bird, because there is a high attrition in these fantastic journeys—but for species at large. The main reason it works is that those places in which the birds arrive, wasted nearly away, usually *do* offer immediate nourishment and shelter. What is more, they offer them nourishment and shelter that was about to get thin back in their breeding grounds.

We naturally think of the breeding country as the bird's home. But for a bird, home is where there is food, comfort, and a species-wide sense of thriving that takes the place of family insularity. When winter hits Montana, Kansas, or Maine, these things vanish. But they can be found in the Yucatán or the greenbelts south of the Sahara, so that is where birds take themselves. We could say that a bird makes the longest trip in nature just to stay at home year-round. And, evidently, the travails of a 10-day flight are easier to survive (as a species) than those of an 8-month winter with no insects, fruits, or seeds.

Scientists are still trying to study specific mechanics of migration—how birds equip themselves to fly so far so fast, how they find their way, and so on—but the larger questions about how birds came to migrate in the first place are argued only in the realm of theory. It is well known that migration is an ancient strategy, that many of the birds of today follow the same routes their ancestors did thousands of years ago. Records in everything from cave paintings to biblical scripture, from Egyptian narrative murals to the notebooks of Aristotle, show that people have long noticed the sudden appearance and disappearance of birds, as well as the passing-through of masses of non-inhabitants on a regular (and obviously tight) schedule. Eating is an ancient strategy, too, after all. But where did the inspiration come from, and how did it turn into such an amazing and precise habit?

One theory says that long ago birds fled south from the creeping onslaught of glaciers that obliterated their food sources in temperate zones; in North America, for example, they would have been pushed into the tropics as most of the continent got icy in the Pleistocene era. When the ice receded, the birds came back, responding to a fundamental homing instinct. They settled, ate well, raised their babies—but when the season began to turn cold and the food started to dwindle, their relatively new tropical instinct asserted itself in turn.

Another theory proposes the opposite: that the birds we see in temperate zones did not originate here, but rather in the tropics. A few (in evolutionary terms this could mean several generations of several species) tried drifting north to places where, in warm seasons, there was plenty of food but less competition than at home. The experiment was fruitful and became a trend, the popularity of which did not ruin the original intent—there was plenty for everyone up north in the summer. In the winter, however, the competition would indeed be too much, so almost everyone zipped back down to the tropics.

These theories, and several others, make a certain amount of sense. The main axis of migration *is* north-south, or temperate-tropical, and the seasonal projections match pretty well for many birds. But there are many more for which the theories hold no explanation. Each migrating species makes a unique commitment to two environments, a route between them, a schedule for the trip, an altitude and time of day for flight, a strategy for sustenance—so many extremely precise variations combined into what looks like one large movement shared with other species, each of which has its own extremely precise variations. The fact is, migration is not really one big behavior most birds have in common. For each species it is a desperate adventure all its own. This is why general theories so far are inadequate.

They are a lot better than many older theories, however—though they are generally less exciting. Scientists, philosophers, poets, and lay naturalists have never been shy about trying to explain the intriguing puzzles of why birds were here today and gone tomorrow. Much of the ingenious guesswork was about where birds went, assuming from the start that they did not fly from, say, northern Germany to southern Egypt—because the little creatures were obviously too frail to cross oceans and deserts. For a long time it was widely believed that birds hibernated in such unlikely places as the bottom of ponds or the inner wood of trees. The author of a scientific paper, published quite respectably in England little more than 100 years ago described in detail how he had unearthed many sleeping swallows near Cambridge!

He can be forgiven, perhaps, inasmuch as he was following a line of confident proclamations that began with Aristotle. The Greek philosopher was actually a naturalist of no mean eye, spotting, for example, the fact that birds are fatter when they migrate—an observation that modern scientists did not catch up with until recently. Aristotle speculated that birds moved around in seasonal shifts and documented the movements by observing which birds came when to Greece. Unfortunately, some of his "observations" of migratory mechanics were rather loony—for example, the claim that larger migrants kindly toted small ones on their backs, as the wee birds were insufficiently hale to make trips on their own.

Aristotle came up with another theory that ran alongside hibernation in explaining what happened to avian residents who suddenly disappeared: transmutation. He said, for example, that redstarts (summer breeders in Greece) did not really leave—they simply turned into robins (winter visitors). Then, in spring, they changed back again—*poof!* He offered as evidence the fact that he had seen birds in transition from one identity to the other (probably a bird in mid-molt). The theory of transmutation was credited for centuries, though its run was not as long as hibernation's.

Once travelers to distant lands began reporting that they had located missing populations of familiar birds, the idea of widespread migration started to catch on. Suddenly there was a sense of some orderly initiative behind the strange departures and arrivals. Naturalists recorded the movements of birds through their areas with precision. Theorists, however, could still get wacky, even when migration was the basis of their ideas: one "scholar" published a paper in 1703 claiming that birds flew not to Africa for the winter—they were far too flimsy for that—but, rather, took a nice, easy, 60-day trip to the moon.

(continued)

In the past 75 years or so, mostly through recording the movements of banded birds, we have discovered truths that are not much easier to believe: hummingbirds that fly thousands of miles nourished mostly by their fat content, ducks that navigate at vast heights through night skies to arrive every year at the same tiny pond on the same date, peregrines that cover 1,800 miles in 24 hours, averaging a speed of 75 mph. The Arctic tern migrates 11,000 miles twice a year, going from the top of the world (the Arctic Circle) to the bottom (Antarctica).

The evidence is incontrovertible: a scientist puts blue band No. 112312-HK on a bird chirping around Indiana; the scientist catches a plane to Mexico four days later; the next day she finds a bird wearing blue band No. 112312-HK larking around Cozumel and simply must conclude that the bird made the trip as rapidly as she did.

The effect of such evidence has been that we finally accept the purely athletic miracle of long migration. We can weigh birds every 6 hours for the 10 days before they leave their breeding grounds and correlate their weight gain with observed changes in their diet. We can analyze blood samples or endocrine secretions and equate certain chemical changes with ruggedness and wanderlust. We can note that migrating species have longer wings than their sedentary cousins. But all of this focus on the physical only heightens our mystification with what we must regard as the mental aspect of migration. How do they know when to leave? How do they find their way?

A sense of when to leave probably starts from the changes in daylight time and the temperature of the environment. When the days begin to get shorter and cooler in autumn and longer and warmer in spring, the bird's pituitary and adrenal glands secrete certain hormones (prolactin and corticosterone) that cause the metabolism to produce and store fat; the hormones, along with the corpulence, initiate a kind of restlessness, too. In the prebreeding migration, other hormones also begin to act on the gonads, swelling the testes and ovaries and, we must assume, igniting many other impulses related to reproduction.

Add to the restlessness and physical readiness an instinctive foreshadowing of the big journey, and the preparation is complete. There are signs all through the breeding cycle that birds are not as absolutely bound to the present as seems indicated by their IQ: they are capable of looking ahead, sensing what is about to happen. The placement and structure of nests, for example, anticipates incubation and chicks. Something as massive as a migration certainly pricks at them before it happens.

How they find their way is not so simple as a few hormones and some fat. Migrating birds spend days and nights in the air above land or sea that may be relatively featureless. Where birds might be able to rely on features of topography, humans are likely to change them, cutting down a forest here or damming a river there; a bird cannot say, "Oh, there's the old elm tree, time to take a left," because the old elm has often been removed in favor of a 6-lane highway. Yet the birds find their way back year after year, often to exactly the same spot they left the previous fall or spring. Some individual birds have returned for more than 30 years to a particular place.

If memorizing a specific route were all there was to it, birds taken to faraway places off the route would be unable to orient themselves and create a new way home. Yet experiments in displacement have shown that birds routinely zip back to their grounds, even when they are subjected to conditions that would bamboozle any sense of orientation humans can understand. A famous example is that of a Manx shearwater from the coast of Wales. The bird was captured, caged, stuck on an airplane that flew 4,000 miles to Boston (the bird was probably kept away from the windows, lest it cheat by peeking), and released. In 12 days it was back in its Welsh nest. There are many stories of famous homing pigeons whose ingenuity and speed compare to this shearwater's, though the distance they travel is usually less amazing; indeed, there are national societies that sponsor competitions between homing birds—which one will get home fastest from the farthest place?

Displacement often occurs in the course of actual migrations, though not usually by the hand of man. Bad weather, especially high-speed wind, will force flocks of migrants off their paths. Some will land and wait out a storm, using the opportunity to refuel with food that may be at hand; others will press on, either re-orienting themselves later and continuing to their destination or, more rarely, improvising and spending a freak season in a strange but supportive environment. The next migration time usually finds these temporarily flexible birds back on course, however.

Scientists have looked everywhere for a clue as to how birds orient and navigate themselves. Do birds really have a sixth sense? If so, it could be found somewhere in the physiology—but there is no evidence of it. Do they have a wondrous memory mechanism that keeps track of every movement made during the trip out and replays the scheme in reverse order during the trip back, independent of ground features? The displacement experiments argue against this idea; so does the ability of newly fledged birds to make precise migrations without being taken over the course in advance. Do birds sense the infinitesimal shifts in the tug of gravity as they approach the equator over the curved surface of the earth or do they sense the pulls of the planet's magnetic field? Probably not, though the idea of magnetic sensitivity has attracted theorists for a century. Several experiments, in which pigeons wore magnetic scramblers and migrated, have been inconclusive, if ingenious.

Now it is generally agreed that birds navigate at least in part by the sun and stars. Their awareness of the sun has long been established, and experiments measuring the perch orientation of caged birds when the sun's position was altered with mirrors has demonstrated that there is a temporal sense integrated with the solar focus to anticipate the sun's motion through the sky. In migration, birds prefer to fly when it is clear or only partly cloudy; fog or complete cloud/cover is usually disorienting, and many birds will land until they can see the sky again. However, *some* birds navigate normally when the reference points in the sky are obscured. Perhaps at these times they *do* rely on a magnetic sensitivity that is otherwise never preferred to visual orientation.

The unavoidable conclusion is that birds navigate by some fantastically complex sensibility that serves the simplest of purposes: to fly hard and fast to a place where there is more food and better weather.

THIS AREA
CLOSED
TO ALL DIGGING
OF CLAMS, QUAHOGS, MUSSELS
AND OTHER MARINE MOLLUSKS
BECAUSE OF POLLUTION

CLOSED AREA NUMBER

Birds and Man:
Whose World Is This?

So far we have looked at birds in detail, as they exist in their natural environments. Not alone, certainly: their lives depend on other forms of life perhaps even more than ours do. But we have looked at them as they are without the benefits or perils of *human* company.

Because human company usually means human intervention, and because human intervention is perilous more often than it is beneficial to birds, their isolation from us is pretty much the ideal situation for them. Unfortunately, like most ideals in nature, this one is increasingly rare in practice. Birds are all over the planet, and so are people. It is inevitable that we meet, in both bonhomie and competition.

If this were a perfect world, the bonhomie would count for a lot. The profound, complex value that an encounter with a wild bird can have for a human being would be regarded as a natural resource worthy of protection. Everyone would want everyone else to have the chance to meet an owl or hummingbird, watch an oriole weave its nest, hear a mockingbird jag through 20 other birds' songs in 5 minutes, or see a falcon patiently feed its eyas. A human action that would threaten a population of birds would be frowned upon. Not all such actions would stop, of course, but the threats to birds would be noticed and solutions would be sought. When the moments of competition arose, the moments of wonder and education would balance our urge to possess whatever it was that we could not share with the birds. There would be a general sense of compromise.

In reality, despite the vigilance of many groups and agencies dedicated to the preservation of wildlife, and their success at stopping a few destructive projects, we take note of only a tiny percent of the damage we do to birds (not individual birds, but whole populations of them). It is hard to imagine that draining a small marsh so a convenience store can be built near a housing development could result in the death of a thousand birds, or that clearing the dead trees from some old woods for firewood might condemn a whole host of woodpeckers and the

Facing page: Arctic tern.

Somebody decided hawks were pests and set a pole trap; this immature red-tail won't get a chance to show it would make a fine controller of vermin.

smaller birds that depend on their holes. These birds will never come back, and they may have nowhere else to go. Shooting a few more ducks than the seasonal limit, buying a pair of parrots from a "discount" dealer in a farmer's market, spraying crops with a hearty dose of insecticide ... these things combine to decimate populations.

For better or worse, we have an immense amount of power to shape the lives we want for ourselves. It is right that we use it. That we also shape the lives of every other creature around us is either a heavy responsibility or an inconsequential nuisance, depending on where one's feelings lie. There are conservationists and wastrels; in between these two polarities are most people, who would save a bird populace if they could, but who also want to have the conveniences of modern life without too much guilt.

Thus it is that most people want to know if birds are doing any *good* in the world—that is, if they are doing any good for *us*. If we are to be so concerned about them, shouldn't there be an accounting of some sort?

Those of us who have grown through experience to cherish wild birds are hard-pressed even to address the question. It strikes an offensive, arrogant note to us. What good are birds? We might as well ask, What good is wordless wonder? What good is the stimulation of an aggressive curiosity that lasts a lifetime? What good is the spirit of respect for the laws of nature and the certainty of our right to discover them in a quest that so far has created every natural science—including medical science? What good is the sense that human beings don't know it all—a sense that tingles every time we see a strange creature solve a problem in a way we never could have imagined—coupled with the confidence that we can, at least, understand the solution once we have seen it?

We wish this kind of evaluation could be enough. We wish that, in response to the question, What are birds *for*?, we could pull a kingfisher out of our pocket and let it dazzle the skeptic simply by its presence, its action, its strange beauty.

But if need be, we can argue that birds do good things for mankind—even demonstrable dollars-and-cents kind of things. We cannot justify the life of every bird in terms of human income; we should never stoop that low, or allow anyone to demand such a ridiculous rationale. We *can* show that birds lead to breakthroughs in the arts and sciences from which we benefit directly. Conversely, we can also show many situations in which man hurts himself by hurting birds—where eliminating them leads to expense, hazard, and a lower quality of life. The consequences are clear: the practical choice between conserving or destroying them is obvious. And although we would prefer that the desire to avoid wiping out birds come from a natural appreciation rather than a calculation of selfish gain, we're glad to show their preservation makes sense. And the birds don't care whether a hectare of forest is saved for them by tree-hugging warbler lovers or by cigar-chewing developers hoping to avoid topsoil runoff onto the 11th green.

Eastern bluebirds reward the house builder by eating lots of caterpillars.

Birds and Pests

In 1958, Mao Tse-tung declared war on the sparrow. China was destitute, and the country's premier saw a resurgence of agriculture as its salvation. Sparrows ate grain that could either sprout or be eaten by people; therefore the birds stood in the way of progress. Mao lumped the sparrow with the fly, the mosquito, and the rat, on a least-wanted list he proclaimed as The Four Evils. The government initiated a nationwide grass-roots program to exterminate these pests, rewarding schoolchildren who bagged large numbers of sparrows and generally creating a sense that birds were The Enemy.

The first result pleased Mao: millions upon millions of sparrows were destroyed. The second result—which took a few years for him to connect to the first—was not so nice: the same crops that had been "saved" from the grain-nibbling birds now succumbed to devastation by hordes of caterpillars.

A sparrow will eat 100 caterpillars a day. Plus maybe a little grain—probably doing about 1 percent of the damage that each one of those caterpillars would do to a crop plant.

The arithmetic is easy to figure. But Mao and his agronomists missed the point, as do so many of today's authorities in high-tech North and South America and Europe. It is easy to cite examples of birds doing us "harm"—of birds eating seeds a farmer has sown, or a bird killing a bird the human hunter feels *he* has the right to kill—and damn birds immediately as pests. Sometimes legal sanction is granted for them to be killed; sometimes—appallingly often—legality is ignored and the cowboy spirit takes over. Let's us take our guns and go blow away some varmints. Blackbird, bye-bye.

Benjamin Franklin wrote a letter to Peter Collinsworth in 1735 on the issue of killing birds because they appeared to be stealing from man: "Whenever we attempt to interfere with the government of the world, we have need to be very circumspect, lest we do more harm than good. In New England they once thought blackbirds useless and mischievous to the corn. They made efforts to destroy them. The consequence was, the blackbirds were diminished; but a kind of worm which devoured the grass, and which the blackbirds used to feed on, increased prodigiously; then finding their loss in grass much greater than their saving in corn, they wished again for their blackbird."

Perhaps the greatest boon birds offer us directly is the control of insect pests. This is an agricultural world; insects are very often the most dire threat to food in an environment. In high-tech countries, farmers spend billions of dollars a year on pesticides that are an expense, not an investment. The toxins don't work consistently, often because pests develop immunities to them, and they have vicious side effects—on wildlife, water, and humans.

Probably as many as 90 percent of the birds in the world eat insects. A swallow or nighthawk may eat thousands a day. Though birds are only one force in the balance of booming versus controlled populations, there is no more formidable foe of the seemingly endless bugs that swarm across cropland in the summer. China is not the only place where the elimination of birds has unleashed a devastation by insects; it happens every year in the United States and Europe in hundreds of places where a swamp has been drained, a forest cut down, a grassland sprayed, or a bounty declared. Suddenly the bugs take over and it is noted too late that the their infestation coincided with the birds' disappearance.

There have been many times in our agricultural history when the reverse has happened: birds have arrived like an airborne army to save us from a localized plague of six-footed pestilence. In the 1870s the Colorado potato beetle was wiping out the tuber crops of the Rocky Mountain states and Mexico, and sweeping eastward with dangerous impunity. Nothing stopped the bugs, and they multiplied with ferocious efficiency: a larva became a beetle in 50 days. One pair of the bugs could produce 60 million of its kind in a single season—and millions of pairs were doing just that.

This went on for several years, until the rose-breasted grosbeak discovered that the potato beetle was rather toothsome. In very little time, flocks of the birds—sometimes eating more than 1,000 larvae and adults per day apiece—had done to the beetles what the beetles were doing to the potato plants, and the crops were free to grow again. It was as if the farmers had discovered a mercenary task force that worked fulltime under all conditions with uncanny determination and cleverness—an army, moreover, that boarded, fed, and paid itself.

Food crops aren't the only commercial resources to receive avian protection from epidemic pest outbreaks. Timber is especially susceptible to many kinds of larvae and beetles. The Engelmann spruce beetle, for example, reigned in Colorado from 1939 to 1952, destroying more than 5 million board feet of the hardwood. But three woodpecker populations—the

The burrowing owl is small, and sometimes takes small prey—but in good numbers.

downy, hairy, and three-toed—suddenly focused on the beetle and gobbled up the wintering broods under the bark of infested trees. The birds cut the pest population by 98 percent in the areas most heavily hit. The epidemic was over.

There are many such tree-saving stories. The heroes are usually resident populations of birds that spend the winter scrounging for food in every crevice or behind every chip of bark. Downy woodpeckers ate up 52 percent of the larvae of the population of codling moths in Nova Scotia apple trees during a long epidemic from 1950 to 1956; this brought the pest population down to a level that could be controlled by normal ecological forces, so that later generations of the bug did not threaten the apple crop. In Mono County, California, chickadees cut a 1961 to 1962 epidemic of lodgepole needle miner by eating 30 percent of the wintering larvae.

Migratory populations save trees, too. Their sudden voracious influx in the spring can negate a rising eruption of pests. Spruce budworms threatened an epidemic in the Adirondacks not long ago, but hordes of returning warblers—tiny birds that drive bird watchers nuts because their dozens of species swarm together—put a stop to them. The warblers zipped merrily about, tweezing larvae from the cocoons spun on the end of spruce branches and feeding them to their nestlings until the larval infestation had been cut by 92 percent.

Scientists estimate that 80 percent of the diet of insect-eating birds consists of harmful species—that is, bugs that damage crops in field, orchard, or forest. When bugs are plentiful, even birds who usually prefer seeds will eat them: a one-week springtime study on 100 acres of grain in North Carolina estimated that sparrows and goldfinches—seed eaters as a rule—were eating

1 million grain aphids per day. Birds do harm crops in many instances, when the wrong bird population meets the right grain at the right time. (Usually the damage is done by an adaptable, "introduced" or non-native species, such as the English sparrow or starling, that has expanded at the expense of another bird driven away from its special habitat by human activities.) But insects are richer food, and a "pest" bird's preference for them might surprise farmers who did not wipe the bugs out first with chemicals.

In the United States—and especially in Europe and Asia, where many traditionalists eschew toxin-tech agriculture's expenses and complicated side effects—there are successful programs aimed at attracting populations of birds to land that will gain in productivity if the birds patrol for pests. Russian scientists have been especially successful at introducing beneficial species into woodlands by moving in adult birds or fledglings who have reached independence. Russian, German, and American programs that place artificial nests in fields or forests have also succeeded in bringing birds to habitats where their appetites will jack up crop yield.

Insects are not the only pests that birds can reduce, of course. Raptors eat a lot of mice and voles and other pestiferous rodents; these animals rarely reach "epidemic" populations. Rabbits do, however. Australia learned earlier this century about the astounding horror of rabbit populations unchecked by natural predators— and is still learning today, as millions of rabbits zoom over the arid land every spring and summer, destroying the precious commodity of green growth that could otherwise be feeding sheep (a major stock industry) and people. There are not enough birds of prey Down Under to handle the rabbits, but localized raptor populations have begun to thrive around the rabbits in many areas. It is one of the few places in the world where eagles are booming, not busting, and where sheep farmers have learned that these great birds are *not* a natural enemy of their flocks.

While the control of animal pests is very dramatic, many farmers would say the most valuable service birds provide is the control of weeds. Sylvester D. Judd, a curmudgeon who wrote several agricultural treatises in the early twentieth century, said: "Even if birds were useful in no other way, their preservation would still be desirable, since in destroying large quantities of weed seed they array themselves on the side of the farmer against invaders that dispute with him, inch by inch, the possession of his fields." (Dr. Judd was not so kind to raptors; in the same piece he says: "The sharp-shinned and Cooper's hawks and the great horned owl are, as everywhere, inimical to the farmer's interests and should be killed at every opportunity.")

Many resident birds eat the seeds of weeds during the winter, nipping a good part of the coming spring's weed crop in the bud; migrants eat weed seeds on the way to their breeding grounds and begin devouring the local seeds as soon as they arrive. Dozens of species of birds live almost entirely on weed seeds. A study some years ago concluded that the quail of Virginia ate 500 tons of weed seed every winter; a similar study by the U.S. Department of Agriculture attributed the destruction of 875 tons to the tree sparrows of Iowa alone. Doves will eat several thousand weed seeds a day, as will meadowlarks, redwing blackbirds, cowbirds, and many sparrows. As they do with insects, birds relentlessly seek their food with thorough attention, going over every inch of ground in their environment, probing everywhere for even microscopic seeds.

Now consider: What happens if every one of those 3,000 to 4,000 seeds a bird eats per day is covered with poison? Perhaps the poison was sprayed to kill the weeds; perhaps it was sprayed to kill insects. In either case, it kills birds.

Birds do not always succumb to pesticides like a cyanide victim in a crime movie; often they live, weakened and polluted, to breed and pass on the effects of the toxins. Chances are their line will not persist for long. Pesticides foul up the delicate hormonal balances that make everything happen at precisely the right time in the healthy bird; they also spoil the materials of the body. Affected birds can be born with spongy

Barn owls are even harder on rats than cats are.

A swarm of birds can destroy many larger swarms of insects around crops.

beaks, blind eyes, no talons, missing wing bones, and all kinds of similarly dooming defects. One widespread effect is the weakening of the process and substances that produce the eggshell. In such cases, the female lays her egg, checks it out, and commences her instinctive care: she settles down on it to incubate. It breaks. She lays another, which also looks okay, and settles gently upon it. It breaks, too. And so on. Pretty soon this bird's family tree has sprung its last bud.

The use of agricultural pesticides is amazingly heavy and widespread. Farmers began using them rather gingerly decades ago, saw dramatic effects, and now depend to a shocking degree upon them; most farmers wouldn't think of planting without spraying several poisons on the things they grow for people to eat. The trouble is, the initial dramatic effects did not last long.

Pesticides weakened the formation of the brown pelican egg at right, and it was crushed in incubation.

160

The poisons stopped working; the farmers increased the amounts. Soon this had no effect; new poisons were added; their amounts were increased when their effects tapered off, too. And on and on and on. In 1950 200,000 pounds of agricultural pesticides were used in the United States. In 1986 the figure had exploded to 1.1 million pounds. It keeps climbing, and chemical firms keep devising new formulas.

The toxins have no place in the natural regulatory system of agriculture (which includes such strategies as the seasons and daylight and the food chain of predation), and thus they are always one-shot interventions. They do not "catch on" and become assimilated into the habits of nature; rather, they intrude and break those habits. Soon everything that was in delicate balance—when and where who eats whom—is out of whack.

The effects are not limited to birds who eat sprayed grain or caterpillars who have consumed sprayed fruit. Pesticides stay in *our* food and run off into the tap water we drink. They cause cancer and a lot of other serious illnesses. The rate of cancer and related fatal diseases—in humans—has risen by something like 70 percent since 1950. Again, the arithmetic is pretty simple.

The most ironic horror in the pesticide mania is that it has all been for nothing. In 1945, before modern toxins gained widespread usage, pests spoiled 1/5 of our national crops. Today—billions of dollars and millions of cancer cases and scores of extinct species later—we lose *the same amount* to pests.

Many toxic chemicals are used not to save produce from destruction, but simply from visual imperfections. Cosmetic prophylaxis: spraying crops with carcinogens so that the oranges don't have any discolored spots, so the apples shine evenly red, so the green beans aren't mottled. One farmer won't stop, because the American public will buy his competitor's grapefruit instead of his, though the unsprayed-but-blemished one tastes exactly as good and is free from poison.

We pay the price in health for our obsession with produce that can star in commercials. Maybe, in some ways, we get what we deserve. But the birds, too, pay a price, species by species. We are killing birds for pretty fruit.

Pets

Watching birds in the wild is one thing. Putting them in a cage in your house is another. Having a bird as a pet gives you the chance to observe one of these distant, skittish creatures close up, as it eats, preens, bathes, sings, and hops around. But caged birds are greatly inhibited. If they cannot fly, they cannot really be birds at all.

Buying a pet bird also supports an industry that may often begin with atrocities in the wild. The owner of your corner pet store may be scrupulous in making certain his canaries and finches and macaws were bred in captivity or imported legitimately and bought from licensed, humane dealers. Unfortunately, there are many more birds that are illegally caught and transported from India, Latin America, Indonesia, Africa, Thailand, and dozens of other tropical places. The world trade in wild birds—as opposed to birds bred specifically for the pet trade—last year amounted to 8 million birds; it is certain that these birds (and many millions more who died in transit) were captured and shipped in ways that a canary owner would revile.

Wild birds are not only big business—a smuggled palm cockatoo would probably fetch from $20,000 to $40,000 and a gyrfalcon would soar to $100,000—they are small business, too. People in developing countries can smear some homemade super-adhesive on a stick, hold it up in a tree, snag a wild bird, yank it off the stick (leaving only a few primary feathers behind, if the bird's lucky), and sell it to a local merchant for a few pennies. The merchant will tape its beak shut, tie its feet with wire, shove it and a couple of others in a cardboard tube that will eventually be hidden in the wheel well of a car crossing a border, and get half a buck for it. And

Sports

Bird watching is probably America's most popular outdoor sport. In the United States in 1985, 134.7 million people spent $14.8 billion observing, photographing, and feeding wildlife, largely birds. More than 25 million people took trips just to observe birds. These figures do not include hunters; there were 5 million of them, spending $1.1 billion pursuing migratory fowl.

The equipment of the bird lover keeps several industries healthy. There are hundreds of companies making bird food, feeders, houses, gadgets to keep squirrels out of feeders and houses, spotting scopes, field guides, and other items used entirely for birding. Bird watchers also buy a lot of binoculars, camera equipment (especially telephoto lenses), and general outdoor gear.

The money and effort they are willing to spend to gain sight of this or that rare bird astound people who haven't caught the bug; many canny birders—who *are* familiar with the mania—have started ancillary industries to help the dedicated ones reach their sightings. For example, there is a subscription service in North Carolina that provides, on a tape recording played over the telephone, up-to-the-hour information on sightings in North America of odd avian visitors. It is nothing for a man in New York to call the hotline, hear that a rare bird has strayed from its usual migratory route into, say, southern Texas, and hop the next plane to El Paso. He will call the hotline for updates on the precise location of the sighting, charter a jeep,

Kids catching bird-watching fever on a refuge in Montana.

head into the desert, see his bird, and hop a plane back. There are several regional Birding Olympics held yearly, in which teams of bird watchers compete to see who can spot the highest number of species in 24 hours in a defined locale, such as the entire state of New Jersey. In Great Britain, manic bird watchers are "twitchers" because they get so frantically excited when a rare one flits in front of their binoculars; they, too, travel the length of the Isles to check out a rumor that a hard-to-find specimen has dropped by.

Bird watchers, jostling the birds they seek, can get in the way of science (not to mention the birds), but in general they contribute a valuable mass of information to people studying the movements of birds. Their dedication—to birds, not just to their lifetime lists—is absolute, and it is understood through an international code of honor that any approach that would disturb a bird whose presence is precarious must not be made, even if a sighting is lost.

Obviously the same cannot hold true for hunters, although there are many hunters who carefully follow bag limits and avoid shooting certain species of waterfowl—when they can identify them in the seconds before a shot. Mostly, however, they simply see ducks and blast away.

Hunting, for all of its carnage, is less of a threat to endangered species than is habitat destruction. However, hunting can have a severe impact on species living in the thin margin between survival and extinction. In many parts of the United States, hunters—most of whom are bird lovers, in their way—are cooperative partners in conservation operations to save wetlands and protect certain species of waterfowl, even when this means they voluntarily forgo legal quotas on such birds. Hunters are very good friends to birds when they appreciate the relationship between restraint and conservation; they want the populations of waterfowl to stay strong. But there are hunters who don't give a hoot, too. They shoot anything that flies, and overreach their quotas whenever possible.

In the past, indiscriminate hunting has accounted for quite a few extinctions. In many countries nowadays, hunting is legally regulated to prevent such wild shooting. But in many others it is not, or regulations are not enforced. Some of these countries are unfortunately situated in the middle of critical migratory routes, and birds passing through are slaughtered by the millions—sometimes for food, sometimes for sport, but often for no useful reason at all.

One such country is Lebanon. It lies on the flight path among three continents, and has been blessed with a great passing-through of birds of all kinds. But great numbers of the troubled, frustrated people of this war-struck land have taken notice only by lifting their machine guns into the air and firing at any flock that flies by. Every year between 15 and 20 million migratory birds are shot down in Lebanon. One hunter alone has shot 50,000 raptors. They are not eaten, sold, collected, or stuffed. They are simply killed. The killing of birds is an expression of the country's anguish, and one feels the horror of that anguish. But the birds are unjust victims, as are those in the rest of the world who await them.

(continued)

A bird needn't even be shot to die from hunting, either. When a duck hunter pulls the trigger of a shotgun, he discharges a spray of lead pellets into the air—and then into the pond, lake, marsh, or river over which his prey is flying. These pellets stick around in the weeds and mud of the bottom, and are eaten by ducks, geese, and swans. Lead, of course, is a poison; a single pellet can kill a bird. Authorities estimate that for every fowl killed, more than 1,000 pellets remain in the environment of its survivors. Thus it is no surprise that 2 to 3 million birds die every year of lead poisoning.

There is yet another extension of the deadliness of shot: scavengers that eat lead-poisoned birds or mammals often ingest lead themselves and are killed. One of the last remaining California condors in the wild died this way. In the United States, a federal ban on lead shot has been put into effect, to eliminate it gradually by the 1990s. However, the ban is being challenged by gun groups—it seems steel shot is slightly less true in its flight than lead shot, and causes more wear to gun barrels. Hunters may win their fight and end up with clean guns, but very few ducks left to shoot.

Two ways to shoot birds.

so on, until the bird (if it is the 1 in 10 that survives the travel) shows up in a pet store in Nebraska or Shropshire or Osaka and sells for $25. It's an easy way to make a tiny bit of money. There are a lot of people who need tiny bits of money, in India, Africa, Thailand, Indonesia, South America, and Mexico—and in the United States, too. There are a lot of birds—though the subtraction of 20 to 80 million a year means perhaps there won't be for long.

Of course, there are ways of supplying birds to the pet trade without brutalizing them or killing off their species. Many of the popular pet species are bred in captivity, setting up an admirably self-sufficient, healthy supply. But many of the most exotic species, including several parrots and cockatoos, cannot be successfully bred in cages. These must be trapped in the wild. Tragically, these are often the species that are already endangered in their habitats—a fact the purchaser rarely knows.

There are national and international regulations regarding the import of "legitimately documented" birds, but they can only be enforced when the birds reach their destination—at which point most of them have already died in their poorly ventilated, overcrowded boxes or cages. Bird dealers regard losses of up to 80 percent of the birds in transit as a regular business condition; it only serves to hike the prices of the birds that survive.

The trapping and trading of many species is forbidden by law in several countries now seeking to protect their birds. But it is easy to "laun-

Birds seized by customs agents on the Mexico-California border. The birds were drugged with tequila, tied with twine, and stuffed into spare tires and side panels of cars.

Black-market birds are big business. This gyrfalcon, protected by law, would fetch more than $100,000 from an unscrupulous falconer.

der" birds in documentation; they can be passed in and out of so many countries on their way to us that even a perfectly legitimate importer may have ambiguous papers, certifying only that their final export was indeed from a country allowed to ship them. Where they came from in the first place is impossible to verify. Some U.S. Customs officials surmise that the illegal trade in exotic birds is as sophisticated and ruthless as the trade in drugs or firearms. Naturally, the beleaguered law-enforcement authorities cannot be expected to drop a cocaine-traffic investigation to chase down some cockatoo smugglers.

Birds and Music

Birds have inspired a lot of art. Their mysteries and physical beauty have nagged painters and poets for as long as there has been paint and language. But the art to which birds have contributed the greatest inspiration is music.

The relationship of birds to human music probably goes back to the earliest song: Did men first raise their voices in imitation of the melodic birds? The vocal music of many ancient cultures—preserved and performed in countries that have no opera halls—is full of bird-song phrases and calls. Songs of ceremony and narrative contain such sounds; songs of communication between distant singers in the jungle or desert obviously imitate the function of bird song as well.

Certainly birds served as models for the invention of the earliest instruments, especially the winds and bowed strings of both East and West. Horns (initially from the heads of animals, reamed and bored; later of brass), pan-pipes, recorders, flutes, oboes, viole da gamba, violins, pipe organs, accordions, and even lutes and harpsichords produce sounds that reveal some sources in bird song. Later reed and brass instruments are probably less directly derived, but nevertheless operate in the same ranges of fidelity to syrinxian vocalization.

The intellect of Western composers soon turned these sounds into structures that had

nothing overtly to do with bird song—though a bird mystic or pedant could argue that every time Mozart wrote a clarinet obbligato he was probably imitating, even unconsciously, some avian grace. The formal punctiliousness of baroque- and classical-period music held no place for mimetic rhapsodies; indeed, the diaries of composers from these times contain more references to the annoying *distraction* of nearby bird song than to the inspiring beauty of such utterances.

European composers in the second half of the nineteenth century began to cop phrases from bird song once more. Usually these phrases were not extended into melody, but served rather as "color" effects. Sometimes they were not necessarily intended to be associated with birds. At other times the sounds were meant to evoke just that association. The programmatic works of many composers directly narrated stories, or at least atmospheres; a bird's sound and identity lent a natural depiction to hundreds of settings. Hardly a Dawn or Nocturne segment of a piece of program music failed to include a flute twittering, a violin singing, or a clarinet lowing. In re-creating the atmospheres of the world—whether it was Richard Strauss doing an Alpine mountainside, Franz Liszt a St. Francis feeding larks, Carl Nielsen the fjords, or Charles Koechlin an evening in the Persian desert—composers were not deaf to the omnipresence of bird song.

The bridge between the programmatic imitation of bird song and the appropriation of its implicit beauty for purely musical purposes coincides in a way with the bridge between the musics of the nineteenth and the twentieth centuries. Composers, like visual artists and writers, began to pick up material from the world around them, turning sounds that had been considered bonded to the things that produced them into unabashed artifice.

Nikolai Rimski-Korsakov of Russia and Leoš Janáček of Czechoslovakia were meticulous notators of bird song, writing down the phrases in standard musical notation. Both used avian melodies in their music, sometimes programmatically (to represent birds), and sometimes integrated without association into the texture of the sound. Rimski-Korsakov was a perfectionist in his reproduction of song, once apologizing for lowering the pitch of a phrase from his pet bullfinch's voice so that it would be within the harmonic range of the violin.

Maurice Ravel was the first of two grand French masters of *musique d'oiseau*. In many of his orchestral pieces, songs, and operas, ingeniously written bird song simultaneously portrays dramatic ambience or action *and* carries on the motivic coherence of the music.

In many of his pieces, the Hungarian Béla Bartók featured atmospheric passages of eerie twitterings, whistling glissandos, and windy rushes —an evocative miasma that came to be generically called night music, full as it was of the natural ambience of insects, nocturnal birds, and masses of air moving in the dark. Many modern composers have used night music in orchestral pieces; one of the best-integrated examples is the opening of Karel Szymanowski's Violin Concerto No. 1. Some composers, such as George Crumb in his string quartet *Black Angels*, have produced it within the instrumental limitations of chamber music.

Igor Stravinsky's mythical *Firebird* is modern music's most famous avian star; her birdliness is evoked with wild power and oddity in his music for this ballet. (The denizens of Peter Ilich Tchaikovsky's *Swan Lake*, however, are doubtless the best-loved balletic birds in music history.) Heitor Villa-Lobos of Brazil created another magical bird as the central spirit of his orchestral tone poem *Uirapuru*, an exotic drama full of fabulous imaginary bird song rendered through instruments indigenous to the Amazon forest.

Perhaps the greatest setting of a vocal narrative about birds is Peter Warlock's *The Curlew*. William Butler Yeats's melancholy lost-love poem takes lonely wing among the spare woodwinds and strings of Warlock's music; the English horn part is especially haunting. The bird of the poem comes alive in this spindrift music as it never did on the page—what was merely a symbol becomes the whole substance and motion of the art.

Many pieces of music in the so-called British pastoral school used birds in evoking the environmental beauties of the countryside. The British composer Ralph Vaughan Williams trailed a beautifully flying bird in his impressionistic concertino *The Lark Ascending*. This piece features an ethereal high violin part that imitates the wheeling grace of flight, not the notes of song. Frederick Delius gave his first clarinetist the most famous two-note phrase in twentieth-century British music, uttered amid the mellifluous orchestral texture of *On Hearing the First Cuckoo in Spring*. The great Frank Bridge—certainly the only iconoclast to wend his thorny way out of the generally tonal-sweet pack of the pastoral school—broke the rules for British avi-music in his long rhapsody *Enter Spring*. This 1927 piece proclaimed the arrival of the green season with shrill, urgent bird song in the woodwinds and thrusting string chords whose brash tonality and sap-raising power startled listeners used to associating spring with sonic pastels of genteel odes.

An even more realistic power is found in the birds of the greatest composer of bird-related music, Ravel's descendant Olivier Messiaen. In the work of no other composer do birds receive such a primary focus, or represent so many layers of significance. Messiaen's later compositions are completely devoted to birds—and through them to God. To Messiaen, a visionary Catholic, birds are the avatars of angels on Earth; their song is thus the holiest sound on the planet, a blessing of direct communication from Heaven. In the *Reveil des Oiseaux*, Messiaen presents an accumulation of birds waking up and singing, one by one, building to an orchestral climax in which more than 20 distinct (in theory, at least) species proclaim the dawn in boisterous, simultaneous chromaticism. In contrast, the seven volumes of the *Catalogue des Oiseaux* are played by solo piano. These are perhaps the best examples in musical literature of accurately rendered bird song integrated with descriptive music portraying habitat and behavior.

Contemporary composers have apparently concluded that after Messiaen, the only progressive step left is the inclusion in their pieces of actual recorded bird song. There are quite a few instances of this, most of them using the bird sounds rather as "found objects" in sonic assemblages. The composers of music that has been dubbed Minimalism—which generally features a regular pulse of rhythm and a long series of repeated phrases (often staccato)—have much in common with the bird trilling his series of variations on the same melody, but the remarkable similarities are probably not intentional.

Another composer whose work uniquely (and probably unintentionally) echoes bird song is Conlon Nancarrow, an American expatriate who composes intricate works for player piano. The music is often incredibly fleet and loud; the tone of the pianos is distinctly twittery in tone; the structures are repetitive, but fresh. The effect is as startling as coming suddenly upon a shrill mockingbird in a calm clearing.

Of course, the by now traditional conscious uses of bird song motifs—for natural atmosphere, textural coloration, dramatic narrative, or pure melody—continues in many of today's composers of art music. In popular music, however—jazz, specifically—birdishness is enjoying a new heyday. The predominance of wind instruments and the zest for flourishes have always led jazzmen toward avian sounds, from the clarinets of early Dixieland to the screeching tenor saxophones of modern free improvisation. In every era jazz artists have a natural affinity with birds: they are devoted to their song, at times compulsively; they are often nocturnal and nomadic; they are set apart from other creatures by the intensity of their life-style. The apotheosis of these traits—indeed, the fountainhead of modern jazz—was Charlie Parker, an alto saxophonist who tore up the music world for a decade and, with his wild lyricism, harmonic ambitiousness, and fleet technique, pointed down roads contemporary musicians are still just beginning to tread. His nickname, which seemed to express everything about him, and became the most universally understood sobriquet in music history, was "Bird."

Aside from the generic bird-song-like playing of clarinetists and saxophonists, and the obvious similarity between a bird riffing on a perch and a musician improvising on a bandstand, bird song popped up in jazz much as it did in classical music: as a kind of atmospheric effect that established a mood and setting. In the late 1920s the Duke Ellington Orchestra stomped around Harlem playing stuff they called jungle music, which featured the growling trombone of Tricky Sam Nanton, the "talking trumpet" of Bubber Miley, and the wailing reeds of Otto Hardwicke and Harry Carney. These players created the shrieks and chatters of tropical birds with dazzling dexterity and amusement. Ellington wrote tunes that were small, exotic fantasias built of dance melodies augmented by the effects of horns and percussion. Later players in the Ellington band, especially trumpeter Cootie Williams and clarinetist Barney Bigard, extended the animal motifs into brilliant solo and ensemble music.

More recently, free jazz led to exploration of new techniques as well as new non-structures. In place of the classic, beautiful tones of beboppers such as Charlie Parker, avant-garde musicians experimented with unorthodox sonorities from split reeds, twisted mouthpieces, odd tunings. For the reed players, this meant a return—sometimes conscious—to sounds that remarkably resemble both bird song and contemporary art music. The music is hardly ever lovely, but neither is much of the world's bird song. A David Murray bass clarinet solo will sound amazingly like Heinz Holliger's *Overtones for the Oboe*, though Murray is improvising as a jazzman and Holliger is at the cutting edge of progressive European classical composers. Incidentally, both of them sound like catbirds.

Coexistence

The biggest measure of our respect for birds is not whether we buy binoculars to watch them or shotguns to shoot them, whether we feed them in our yard or cage them in our homes, whether we trust them to kill the bad bugs on our land or bypass them to poison their food and water with pesticides. It is whether or not we can share the planet with them.

To human beings, every spot on earth is a potential place to live. We are amazingly adaptable, and our architecture allows us to inhabit mountaintops, swamps, deserts, and islands, establishing through artificial structures a homeostasis, a permanent comfort zone: we can make it 72°F *anywhere*.

Birds, too, have their means of achieving homeostasis. They migrate, following the comfort zone as it passes south and north with the seasons. This is a tremendously brave and ingenious way of staying "at home." They have discovered places they can live in as many different spots on earth as we have, and have made a home in most every natural environment.

But although we see a lammergeier on Mt. Everest and a kite in the Everglades, we should not conclude that birds in general are as adaptable as humans. Man is one species; birds are nearly 9,000. A Masai warrior from Africa and a Finn could sit down at the same table in a Denver house and eat the same food quite comfortably. Not so the lammergeier and the kite. Each species of bird has adapted itself to a very specific kind of environment that provides very specific opportunities to nest, eat, and hide. To remove the bird from this environment is to destroy it.

But it is most often the environment that is destroyed first. *The single largest cause of extinction of wildlife is the destruction of habitat.* Extinctions through slaughter may be more well-known—the dodo, the passenger pigeon, the European bison, the Steller's sea cow, all of whom we wiped out by picking them off one by one out of hunger, sport, or mindless meanness. But many more animals have been lost through the cutting of forests, and the dam is far deadlier than the bullet.

It is hard for us to be fully aware of what is at stake for a whole population of birds when we decide to build a new road through the middle of a woods, or put a storage warehouse in a grassy field on the edge of town. We see no harm in taking a strip down the middle of the woods and leaving the rest or clearing a weedy plot for a few low storage sheds. When a dam is proposed, we look at curvy, trickling streams that will be turned into straight, roaring rivers, and fail to understand how *more* water can be bad for birds that now choose to live near a *little* of it.

The fact is that *any* change is a threat to the balance of plant and animal lives in a specific environment, even a change that might seem to us an improvement for wild creatures. A roaring river supports an entirely different chain of substances and creatures—from plants to insects to reptiles to mammals to birds—than a meandering stream. Eventually the river may gather to itself a flourish of wildlife—but chances are it will be completely different life forms from what was originally there. Chances are, too, that it will be wildlife of a commoner, more adaptable variety—the secondary, mop-up-crew species that take over when more slowly evolved species fade with their environment. These more adaptable creatures often proliferate unilaterally and become tremendous pests, because those species that prey on them tend to be among the slow-and-specific developers that are now gone.

Everything in an environment matters to someone higher up the food chain. When soil runoff from a thinning forest silts riverbeds upstream and eradicates one kind of underwater weed in a bay, the crustacea that depend on the weed, the fish that depend on the crustacea, and birds that depend on the fish *and* shellfish will also be wiped out, causing the boom of certain pest fish and marsh insects, and so on. You might think all you have done by cutting some trees is dispose of a few woodpeckers on the site. Instead you end up with a plummeting shellfish

This penguin has its habitat to itself—for the time being. Fewer and fewer birds are so lucky.

Products

In the United States we are quite familiar with the world's most commercially productive bird, the domestic fowl, or chicken. Billions of these birds are raised around the world for their eggs, feathers, droppings, and meat, supporting many industries as diverse as sausage packagers and pillow manufacturers. In many impoverished areas a few chickens means the difference between a family's survival and its starvation.

After the domestic fowl, perhaps the most productive birds are several species of tropical colony-nesting seabirds, including gannets, boobies, pelicans, and cormorants. These birds are not eaten, nor are their eggs—yet they are absolute gold in the export economies of the countries they inhabit, as well as in the domestic agrarian sectors. What these birds provide is not cultivated, and the birds don't need special management or supervision to keep them on the job. They make it all by themselves if we just leave them alone: a mountainous amount of excrement.

The excrement—called guano—is not just any old cloacal effluvium. Because of the anchovetas upon which the birds feed (and because of the diatoms eaten by these fish), guano is amazingly rich in nitrogen and phosphorous, which do not leach in the rocks or evaporate in the dry climates of their island habitats. The guano accumulates and does not spoil; on some islands it is 100 feet deep. The chalky stuff is mined as if it were a mineral and packaged for use as fertilizer. There is no better one in the world.

Guano has had a long run at the top of the fertilizer industry. Between 1848 and 1875, the United States and Europe imported more than 200 million tons of it. How-

industry, rivers full of carp instead of salmon or bass, and a plague of gnats and mosquitoes.

Once we accept the fact that birds live in *particular* places for *precise* reasons, and cannot just go somewhere else when we evict them, we can begin to see how deeply they are affected through our exploitation of the land. In the United States we have altered the land in many irrevocable ways: the conversion of the great prairies into farmland, the eradication of the ancient forests in the East, the development of the shorelines, the redirection of countless rivers and streams, the draining and filling of natural wetlands ... and on top of such topographical revision are

the chemical changes to every cubic foot of air and water.

It must be remembered, too, that the survival of a bird depends not just on one environment, but on several. There is a wintering ground, a breeding ground, and a migratory route in between. Severe changes to any of these may threaten the bird. Ornithologists in North America have been increasingly concerned in recent years as they've noticed a decline in the numbers and diversity of birds that breed here but spend their winters in Latin America. This includes more than 1/3 of the six hundred and fifty bird species that breed in the United States. A visit to the ever, the supplies began to dwindle in the early twentieth century, and South American countries moved to protect the birds and their nesting grounds from overuse. The islands now are bird sanctuaries, and the removal of guano is calculated for replenishment. A hundred cormorants produce about a ton in one year; there are millions of birds. The largest threat to the guano industry now is the fishermen who net anchovetas, which are then ground into fish meal—also a major cash crop. If the birds don't get enough to eat—and the fishermen are making serious depletions in the anchoveta population—they obviously cannot produce the guano.

There is nothing precious about ostrich dung, but that's practically the only part of the world's largest bird that is not useful to the ranchers who have brought it back from the brink of danger in Africa. Its eggs (equal in volume to 24 fowl eggs), meat (thick enough to produce steaks), and even esophagus are eaten; its skin is used for leather goods (especially popular in Texas for cowboy boots), its feathers have come back into style for hats and boas, and its sweetbreads are ground into a popular kind of garlic sausage.

Ostrich-ranching is an old method of conservation and exploitation, dating back to the 1830s. The birds, especially their feathers, meant big money: from 1910 to 1913, exported feathers brought $76 million (about $800 million in today's money) to South Africa, seat of most ostrich-ranching. But when ostrich feathers went out of style around 1915—because the hats they adorned blew off in newfangled roofless automobiles and snug pillboxes and cloches replaced them—the industry fell apart, the ranches were shut down, and the bird's wild population began to dwindle. But the bird survived its time out of fashion and is now the beneficiary of the cyclical nature of style: ostrich feathers (at $70 a pound) have made a comeback, and so have the ranches.

southern wintering countries made clear the cause of the disappearance: in many of the tropical countries, the vast expanses of rain forest are being slashed and burned at a madcap pace, with thousands of square miles burning around the clock at any given time.

Behind the destruction of the forest is the belief that the creation of new farmland is economically beneficial. But the reality is more bitter: the land will very likely support meager crops for a couple of years, at best, leaving the would-be farmers with wasteland tracts. We are fostering the "greenhouse effect" in the depletion of great resources of vegetation by filling the atmosphere with carbon dioxide (and other smoke pollutants) instead of preserving the vast conversion factories that used to *consume* carbon dioxide and produce oxygen in vast amounts.

These are the problems for people. The problems for birds are obvious. Many of our summer birds have nowhere to go for the winter. They become wanderers, their annual cycle is disturbed, and they are dying off rather quickly. Take, for example the Kentucky warbler, who breeds in the Potomac River basin in Virginia. The habitat there has remained unchanged for years. Under such conditions, ornithologists expect about 75 percent of banded birds to return

Old forest falls to the impetuous chain saws of clear cutting in Washington.

each year, but recently the Kentucky warbler migration has dropped off alarmingly—only 30 percent of the banded birds are returning. It's not because they have found a nicer spot farther downriver in Virginia; it's because the tropical forests in which the bird used to pass its winters have been burned or cleared to the ground.

The story is the same for the Bachman's warbler that winters in Cuba, the Swainson's warbler that winters in the Antilles, and a host of other songbirds that arrive at the end of an exhausting migration south to find their homes eradicated. And of course we are not exactly standing still up here in the northern breeding grounds either: our forests are being cut into parcels, our grasslands have virtually vanished,

we are draining wetlands and irrigating desert. So the smaller numbers of birds that do manage to return find themselves—at the end of *another* exhausting migration—faced with fast-food stores or alfalfa fields laced with poison instead of woods or plains. California, for example, has lost 92 percent of its original 5 million acres of wetlands. It has lost a lot of its migratory birds as well, and those that survive are crowding into the shrinking refuges, where they are particularly susceptible to epidemics of botulism and cholera.

Now that our prairies are gone, the largest current destruction of habitat comes from the fragmentation of forests. When we cut down part of a forest and surround it with development or at least a different landscape, we are creating an island. The creatures that used to live in the forest collapse onto the island, which sets up an artificially dense and competitive environment that is fatal for many birds. Also, predators and parasites are now pushed into the same space with new victims, which used to avoid them in more open spaces. Nests are especially vulnerable to brood parasites and egg thieves; unluckily, most of the migrants from Latin America and the Caribbean produce only one clutch per season. If it is spoiled, that's it for the year: no offspring.

Not everyone loses in this situation. Cowbirds, grackles, blue jays, foxes, and snakes love the new opportunities, the way a rural pickpocket loves the new amusement park that draws prey to its turf. The continued presence of birds and wildlife—like the continued presence of token forest—deludes us, so that the problem doesn't *look* as bad as it really is. We hear and see birds, spot a fox and a deer, catch a turtle or a garter snake—and conclude that those woods the developers left us are a virtual wildlife sanctuary. We are unaware that we are losing diversity and yielding ground to the most common species that actually help man the least. A normal, healthy warbler population eats a lot more insects than a normal cowbird population. As we lose our songbirds, we will very likely see an explosion of insects that are usually at their most vulnerable larva stage when the songbirds arrive in the

As the Brazilian rain forest is destroyed, so are many birds who breed in North America.

Flying for Thrills

In the old days, falconry, like other forms of hunting, was above all a means of getting meat. A laird's hunters could shoot a boar with an arrow or trap a hare in a noose, but catching doves or partridge on the wing was too much to ask of a human. So it was asked of another bird: a raptor for whom such fare was natural prey.

Birds ranging from small sparrow hawks to great eagles were trained, entirely through the withholding and granting of food; they learned to sit on a falconer's hand, fly from it, and return to it. They were kept slightly hungry, so that the falconer's bribes were always accepted—and, finally, so that when they were flown they would make the considerable effort required to seek and kill prey on their own. A raptor will not kill for its own sport, but only because it must eat. Nor will it fetch its prey back to the falconer; it must be pried away before it has eaten its fill. The slightly mangled partridge or squab could then find its way to the laird's table.

Today falconry, like hunting, is nothing but a killing sport, in which the securing of a dead animal is secondary to the thrill of intimacy with wild creatures and terrain. Falconers use much the same equipment their forebears used, and fly birds in the same way. Because birds of prey are so delicate, so skittish, and so irredeemably wild, the breeding and training of them is incredibly detailed, difficult, and expensive. For the falconer, part of the thrill of releasing a bird to hover high and stoop to the kill is the wonder: Will it come back?

It is illegal almost everywhere in the world to capture wild birds of prey for falconry without licenses that are carefully controlled. There is a pricey trade in smuggled raptors—a peregrine falcon will fetch at least $50,000—but most legitimate falconers prefer to support efforts to breed the birds in captivity. This is more economical, but most importantly it establishes independent populations of birds that are endangered in the wild. Because falconers are such experts in the handling and care of these birds, they have been leaders in evolving techniques of breeding that may lead not only to a self-sufficient supply of sporting birds, but also to a source of birds that can be returned to the wild to strengthen waning species.

Not all raptors are good for sporting. Owls are completely unsuitable, and eagles are too slow, lazy, and irregular in their appetites. Buteos take well to humans and are good for hunting game on the ground—rabbits, squirrels. Accipiters are moody,

spring. Farmers will notice, with chagrin. Pesticide companies will profit. And we will all wonder at the paucity and prices of produce at the grocery store. The worst of it might be what shows up when we go to the doctor for a checkup.

What can we do? As mentioned earlier, we cannot expect people to become suddenly enraptured with the survival of birds they never notice in their lives anyway. We cannot expect good-looking plans for a housing development to be scrapped because a few warblers will turn into lots of blue jays. We cannot hope that a dam that would give jobs to 300 people for a couple of years will be held up until a population of endangered raptors is relocated from desert that will turn into a lake. Man, like all finicky, and small, but the goshawk is a good enough hunter that many falconers put up with these difficulties.

The most exciting prey for a falconer is a bird in flight, so the most highly cherished species is the peregrine falcon, which circles high and falls on lower-flying birds in a dramatic stoop. Gyrfalcons, the largest of the Accipiters, are also prized, but they require a forbidding amount of space and exercise because of their size, power, and method of hunting. Merlins hunt very well off the fist, and pursue small birds with great elan. The hobby, a small European falcon, seems perfect for the sport, but as soon as it is released for the hunt it begins to snack on insects, and thus isn't as lusty in pursuit of prey as the falconer would like. The zest of a good chase is what the falconer seeks—as long as the chase does not take the bird away over the next hill, for good.

A peregrine on a falconer's fist, held by its jesses.

creatures, thinks of himself first.

But man stands to lose in his foolish devotion to short-term gratification. As we have demonstrated, birds are very good for man. When we share the land with them, we profit. It is unfortunate, however, that these subtle, complex, and long-term benefits are too often overlooked, in favor of a shiny new project.

We cannot stop the growing splendor of our technology. But we can take stock in advance of what we may lose if things are done carelessly. We needn't even change our values, though undoubtedly a bit less man-made selfishness would increase our enjoyment of the world. We need only accept the silent laws of nature that are already operating in our favor, and make our

An Avian Recipe for Health

In the 1950s, a bug called the barbeiro was ravaging impoverished Brazilians—especially children—by the millions, right in the snugness of their mud huts. The insect lived in the inevitable cracks that laced adobe walls, and bit hut dwellers on the neck and face, infecting them with a microorganism that damaged heart muscles and led to fierce illness and sudden death. By 1957, more than 4 million people had died.

There seemed to be no way to exterminate the insects, and Chagas' disease (named after the physician who discovered the microorganism) was becoming epidemic. Then Dr. Mario Pinotti, head of the national Department of Endemic Diseases, happened one night to recall that as a boy he and his friends used to throw stones at the dried-mud nests of the Brazilian ovenbird, with no effect: the nests were surprisingly stout and did not crack. Pinotti got some ovenbird nests and analyzed their composition. He found that they contained a secret ingredient—cow dung—that was not used in the mud of human huts. Could this be the source of their impermeability?

Thinking that eliminating cracks might eliminate barbeiros more effectively than trying to exterminate them, Pinotti initiated a project to patch the cracked walls of huts with mud made according to the ovenbird's recipe, cow dung and all. A pilot study of 2,000 homes showed that six months after being patched with dung mud, *none of the huts* contained the insects anymore—though 98 percent of them had been infested before the sealant was applied. The dung was odorless in its mix, and did not launch any new infections, so the ovenbird's mud was immediately prescribed for 200,000 huts in 1958, and 2.5 million in the next few years. The epidemic of Chagas' disease was curtailed, saving millions of lives. Thus, the ovenbird is one of the greatest heroes in the history of public health in Brazil.

---

plans with these laws in mind. These laws of nature, after all, are the very forces that have allowed us to evolve to our present eminence.

A close study of birds reveals useful lessons for humans. Birds react more intensely to things that disturb or encourage them, but these things will also reach us. They demonstrate losses or gains to which we will soon be subjected. Just after World War II, farmers began using pesticides in huge amounts with the assumption that they weren't hurting anyone; 40 years later the escalation of terminal diseases in humans shows they were wrong, and we are finally getting alarmed. But birds showed us first: it was in raptor populations in the late 1940s and early 1950s that the effects of DDT were first assessed as a public health issue, leading to legislative controls. So it may be with the greenhouse effect, and the wholesale destruction of tropical forests—or any of a number of human actions and their unknown environmental consequences.

Has the creature we have always turned to for an expression of exultation and freedom through song and grace become the clinical harbinger of our woes? It needn't be so as long as we keep our eye on the birds, as we always have, and make certain they stay around to express our better selves.

Logs clog waterways.

179

Gannet.

Bibliography

Books

Allen, G. M. *Birds and Their Attributes.* New York: Dover, 1962.

Armstrong, E. A. *Bird Display and Behavior.* New York: Oxford University Press, 1942.

———. *The Folklore of Birds.* London: William Collins Sons & Co., 1958.

Austin, E. S. *Birds That Stopped Flying.* New York: Random House, 1969.

Bologna, G. *Simon and Schuster's Birds of the World.* Edited by John Bull. New York: Simon & Schuster, 1978.

Boswell, J. *Birds for All Seasons.* London: BBC Publications, 1986.

Broun, M. *Hawks Aloft.* Kutztown, PA: Kutztown, 1960.

Burnie, D. *Bird.* New York: Alfred A. Knopf, 1988.

Burroughs, J. *Locusts and Wild Honey.* Boston: Houghton, Osgood & Co., 1879.

Burton, R. *Bird Behavior.* London: Granada, 1985.

Cade, T. J. *The Falcons of the World.* Ithaca, NY: Comstock/Cornell University Press, 1962.

Campbell, B., and E. Lack, eds. *A Dictionary of Birds.* Vermillion, SD: Buteo Books, 1985.

Cavagnaro, D. *Feathers.* Portland, OR: Graphic Arts Center, 1982.

Cruikshank, A. D., and H. G. Cruikshank. *1001 Questions Answered About Birds.* New York: Dover, 1976.

Decker, D. J., and G. R. Goff, eds. *Valuing Wildlife.* Boulder, CO and London: Westview Press, Inc., 1987.

Ehrlich, P. R., D. S. Dobkin, and D. Wheye. *The Birder's Handbook.* New York: Simon & Schuster, 1988.

Ford, E. *Birds of Prey.* London: BT Batsford, 1982.

Freethy, R. *How Birds Work.* Poole and Dorset, Eng.: Blandford Press, 1982.

Halliday, T. *Vanishing Birds.* New York: Holt, Rinehart & Winston, 1978.

Harris, J. T. *The Peregrine Falcon in Greenland.* Columbia and London: University of Missouri Press, 1981.

Harrison, H. H. *A Field Guide to Birds' Nests.* Boston: Houghton Mifflin, 1975.

———. *A Field Guide to Western Birds' Nests.* Boston: Houghton Mifflin, 1979.

Hudson, W. H. *Adventures Among Birds.* New York: E. P. Dutton, 1920.

———. *Birds and Man.* London: Longmans, Green & Co., 1901.

———. *The Bird Biographies of W. H. Hudson.* Santa Barbara, CA: Capra Press, 1988.

Johnson, W. *The Journals of Gilbert White.* Cambridge, MA: M.I.T. Press; London: Routledge & Kegan Paul, 1970.

Kress, S. W. *The Audubon Society Handbook for Birders.* New York: Charles Scribner's Sons, 1981.

Leahy, C. *The Bird Watcher's Companion.* London: Robert Hale, 1982.

Mackenzie, J. P. S. *Birds in Peril.* Boston: Houghton Mifflin, 1977.

McElroy, T. P., Jr. *The Habitat Guide to Birding.* New York: Nick Lyons Books, 1974.

Mead, C. *Bird Migration.* New York: Facts on File, 1983.

Middleton, A. L. A. and C. M. Perrins. *The Encyclopedia of Birds.* New York: Facts on File, 1985.

Mills, E. A. *Bird Memories of the Rockies.* New York: Houghton Mifflin, 1931.

Mitchell, A. W. *The Enchanted Canopy.* New York: Macmillan, 1986.

Nilsson, G. *The Bird Business.* Washington, D.C.: Animal Welfare Institute, 1981.

Pasquier, R. F. *Watching Birds.* Boston: Houghton Mifflin, 1977.

Peterson, R. T. *A Field Guide to the Birds.* Boston: Houghton Mifflin, 1980.

Pettingill, O. S., Jr. *Ornithology in Laboratory and Field.* Minneapolis, MN: Burgess, 1970.

Robbins, C. S., B. Bruun, and H. S. Zim. *Birds of North America.* New York: Golden Press, 1966.

Shrubsall, D. *Birds of a Feather.* Unpublished letters of W. H. Hudson, Moonraker Press, 1981.

Stefferud, A. *Birds in Our Lives.* U.S Department of the Interior. Washington, D.C.: U.S. Government Printing Office, 1966.

Terres, J. K. *Discovery: Great Moments in the Lives of Outstanding Naturalists.* Philadelphia: J.B. Lippincott, 1961.

————. *How Birds Fly.* New York: Doubleday, 1968; Harper & Row, 1987.

————. *The Audubon Society Encyclopedia of North American Birds.* New York: Alfred A. Knopf, 1980.

Welty, J. C. *The Life of Birds.* Philadelphia and London: W. B. Saunders, 1962.

Zim, H. S., and I. N. Gabrielson. *Birds, A Guide to the Most Familiar American Birds.* New York: Golden Press, 1956.

Periodicals

Barnes, J. "Raven Rolling on Ground to Avoid Peregrine." *British Birds* 79 (5) 1986:252.

Bashline, J. "Feather Merchants." *Field and Stream,* Mar. 1985, 47–48.

Beehler, B. M. "Observations on the Ecology and Behavior of the Pale-billed Sicklebill." *Wilson Bulletin* 98 (4), 1986:505–515.

Begley, S., G. C. Lubenow, and M. Miller. "Silent Spring Revisited?" *Newsweek,* July 14, 1986.

Boling, R. "Battered Birds of Lebanon." *Audubon,* Jan. 1986, 36–39.

Browne, S. "Is There a Black Duck in Your Future?" *The Conservationist,* Sept./Oct. 1983, 42–45.

Calderazzo, J. "Saving China's Birds." *Audubon,* Nov. 1985, 48–53.

Cohen, R. R. "Swallows Taking Insects from Pond Surfaces." *Wilson Bulletin* 98 (3), 1986:483–484.

Darrow, H. N. "Spiraling Behavior and Use of Thermals." *Florida Field Naturalist* 11 (2), 1983:35–39.

Di Silvestro, R. L. "How Many Birds Perished in Goldfish Farm Holocaust?" *Audubon,* Sept. 1988, 14.

Ehrlich, P. R. "Winged Warning." *Sierra,* Sept./Oct. 1988, 57–61.

Gaston, T. "Down to the Sea." *Natural History,* July 1988, 26–28.

Graham, F., Jr. "Confrontation in the Skies." *Audubon,* Jan. 1983, 22–24.

————. "Returning the Terns." *Audubon,* Jan. 1985, 14–17.

Havill, E. "The Marvel of Flight." *Blair and Ketchum's Country Journal,* Apr. 1984, 45–53.

Jenkins, F. A., Jr., K. P. Dial, and G. E. Goslow, Jr. "A Cineradiographic Analysis of Bird Flight: The Wishbone in Starlings Is a Spring." *Science,* Sept. 16, 1988, 1495–1498.

King, J. R. "Fault Bars in the Feathers of White-Crowned Sparrows." *AUK* 101 (1), 1984:168–169.

Laycock, G. "Doing What's Right for the Geese." *Audubon,* Nov. 1985, 119–133.

Leo, J. "Looking for Mr. Goodbird." *New York,* June 10, 1985, 57–65.

Livezey, B. C. "Mechanics of Steaming in Steamer-Ducks." *AUK* 100 (2), 1983:485–488.

Mendez, R. A. "Ant Acid Spells Relief." *Natural History,* May 1984, 93, 101–103.

Moreau, R. E. "Incubation and Fledging Periods of African Birds." *AUK* 57, 1940:313–323.

Munn, C. A. "The Real Macaws." *Animal Kingdom,* Sept./Oct. 1988, 20–33.

New York Times, "The Burning of Rondonia." Aug. 29, 1988, A18.

New Yorker, "The Largest Cockatoo." Apr. 22, 1985, 36–38.

Page, J. "Clear-cutting the Tropical Rain Forest in a Bold Attempt to Salvage It." *Smithsonian,* Apr. 1988, 107–116.

Preston, C. R., and Mosley and Mosley. "Green-backed Heron Baits Fish with Insects." *Wilson Bulletin* 94 (4), 1986:613–614.

Revkin, A. "How Do Wings Work?" *Science Digest,* Oct. 1983, 91:84.

Rice, E. K. "The Palm Cockatoo." *Animal Kingdom,* Sept./Oct. 1988, 55.

Riley, L. "Birdman of the Great Swamp." *Blair and Ketchum's Country Journal,* June 1985.

Rosenbauer, T. "A Salmon Delights in Gaudy Colors." *Audubon,* Sept. 1987, 65–72.

Short, L. L., and J. F. M. Horne. "Answering the Call of the Honeyguide." *International Wildlife,* Mar./Apr. 1988, 43–44.

———. "I Saw It!" *International Wildlife,* Mar./Apr. 1987, 22–23.

Snell, R. R. "Underwater Flight Observed of Long-tailed Duck." *IBIS* 127 (2), 1985:267.

Steinhart, P. "Empty the Skies." *Audubon,* Nov. 1987, 72–95.

———. "Trouble in the Tropics." *Natural History,* Dec. 1983/Jan. 1984, 16–20.

Stuller, S. "Keeping an Eagle Eye on Our Feathered Friends." *Sports Illustrated,* Aug. 22, 1988, 6–7.

Thomsen, J. B., and G. Hemley. "Bird Trade. . . . Bird Bans." *TRAFFIC* (U.S.A.) 7, nos. 2, 3, Feb. 1987.

Time, "Cow-Dung Cure." June 23, 1958, 66.

Tomback, D. F. "Foraging Behavior of a Cross-billed Nutcracker." *Western Birds* 12 (3), 1982:137–138.

Turnbull, S. "Osprey Catching Two Fish in One Dive." *British Birds* 79 (5) 1986:502–503.

van Vuren, D. "Aerobatic Rolls in Courtship and Play." *AUK* 101 (3), 1984:620–621.

Wilcove, D. S., and R. F. Whitcomb. "Gone with the Trees." *Natural History,* Sept. 1983, 82–91.

Wilson, R. P. "Prey Seizing in African Penguins." *Ardea* 74 (2), 1986:211–214.

Whitson, M. A. "Clown of the Desert." *National Geographic,* 163, no. 5, May 1983, 694–702.

Younghusband, P. "Down on the Ostrich Farm." *International Wildlife,* Sept./Oct. 1984, 52–60.

Index

(Numbers in italics refer to illustrations.)

Photo and Illustration Credits